Kaleidoscope: Life's Meaningful Reflections

Volume One

That's ENUF!!!

Vanessa Conaway Pace

Pace Publishing
Post Office Box 2187
Lynnwood, WA 98036

www.pacepublishing.com

Kaleidoscope: Life's Meaningful Reflections
Volume One: That's ENUF!!!
Black and White Paperback Edition

Prose, Poetry, Music, and Design Created By:

Vanessa Conaway Pace

Cover Design by: milagraphicartist@gmail.com

ISBN Number: ISBN-13: 978-0-9704373-4-1
               ISBN-10: 0-9704373-4-X

Copyright © 2018 by: Pace Publishing
                       Post Office Box 2187
                       Lynnwood, WA 98036 USA

                       www.pacepublishing.com

Printed/Duplicated in the United States of America. All rights to this book and its design are reserved to the Author under International Copyright Law. No part of this design, these contents and/or cover may be reproduced in whole or in part in any form by any means—electronic, mechanical, photocopy, video or audio recording, or any other—except for brief quotations in printed reviews, without the prior express written consent of the Publisher.

About The Author

Vanessa Conaway Pace is a direct descendant of the Welsh Bards, and is an Award-Winning Poet, "with the distinction of Poet Fellow, in honor of creative work", by Nobel House, London, England, 2007. (See poems page 97 and 179.) This current Volume is the first in the "**Kaleidoscope**" Book/Audio/Video Series of "Life's Meaningful Reflections".

She is an international singer with 9 albums (in 5 languages) to her credit, is Host and Producer of two long-running weekly half-hour television series, along with numerous television specials, and is a frequent presenter at conferences and seminars.

Vanessa is creator of the voice training books and audio series entitled "Managing Your Computerized Voice Box", and is Co-Author of "For The Love Of Children: A Guidebook for Early Childhood Education".

As a Teacher of the Creative Arts, Vanessa Coaches Voice in her Studio in Lynnwood, WA, and internationally via electronic media. She holds a Bachelor of Arts Degree in Music Performance, and maintains a varied performing career ranging from Opera to Broadway.

"My Life's Kaleidoscope is ever-changing: ...: Writing, Singing, Teaching, Coaching, Creating, Concertizing, Producing books/greeting cards/albums, ...,

"..., Learning/Researching/Lecturing about The Power of Sound and the scientific and esoteric basis thereof, ...,

"What a wonderful world we have to explore, and understand, and subdue!"
Vanessa

Other Books and Materials By This Author

"For The Love Of Children: A Guidebook for Early Childhood Education";
with Marguerite Laskares and Tamra Pace

"Secrets of Voice Development"
for Speakers and Singers;
Course Numbers 1 and 2

"Rejoice! A Celebration of Christmas" Music Cd

"He's Alive!!!": Gospel Music Cd, Sung in English

"El E Viu": Gospel Music Cd, Sung in Romanian

"Yazutse!!!: Gospel Music Cd, Sung in Kenyarwandan
(the native language of Rwanda)

"The Master's Voice": Hymns in Classical Settings,
Sung in English

"Lodiamo Dio": Hymns in Classical Settings,
Sung in Italian

"Din Dragostea": "To Romania With Love",
Hymns in Classical Settings,
Sung in Romanian

"Great Classical Arias and Duets":
with Finnish Coloratura Mezzo Soprano
Helena Niemispelto;
Sung in English, Italian, Finnish, and Latin

www.pacepublishing.com

Dedication

*To Mother and Daddy,
Freeda and George Conaway,
who gave me a love for words,
and their meaning,
and their power,
and their expressive beauty.*

*Thanks for all those hours
when you read to me,
and encouraged me,
and helped me
to Be Who I AM!*

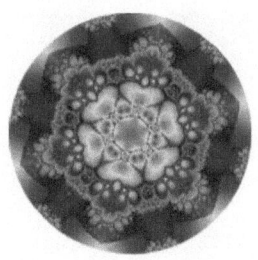

www.pacepublishing.com

Acknowledgements

To the Authors,
    Whose books
        I took from the shelf,
            Who helped Me
                To see
                    *The True **Me***
                        In Myself,

And to all
    Who have searched
        For an answer
            Or two
                To the questions
                    Of Life,
                        Let Me say
                            Unto You

A deeply felt
    "Thanks!",
        For sharing Your "stuff",
            And enriching
                Our Energy Pool,

        For We've learned
            Truths from You
                That enlightened Our "zoo"
                    With advancements
                        That make others
                            Drool!!

And to those
>   Who helped fill
>   >   Our Technology Pool
>   >   >   With the gadgets
>   >   >   >   We need to create,

Let Me say
>   A big "Thanks!"
>   >   For You belong
>   >   >   To the ranks
>   >   >   >   Of the folks that I think
>   >   >   >   >   Are just GREAT!!

And to families
>   Who gave Us
>   >   Some time out
>   >   >   To muse,
>   >   >   >   So We'd garner
>   >   >   >   >   Some thoughts
>   >   >   >   >   >   That the whole world
>   >   >   >   >   >   >   Can use! ...!

And to **You**,
>   Who will open
>   >   Your great Heart,
>   >   >   And Your Mind,
>   >   >   >   As We ponder these thoughts
>   >   >   >   That I've penned,
>   >   >   So, together We'll blend
>   >   >   >   Into one giant "Friend"
>   >   >   >   >   Full of Laughter
>   >   >   >   >   >   And Love
>   >   >   >   >   >   >   To the end!!!

>   >   >   >   >   Vanessa Conaway Pace
>   >   >   >   Lynnwood, Washington, October 23, 2013

My deep gratitude also goes to my friend and colleague, Marguerite Laskares, who has taken time from her own brilliant work in Early Childhood Education*, to provide invaluable editorial and production assistance on this Volume.

Many thanks for all those happy creative hours!!!

*See "For The Love Of Children: A Guidebook For Early Childhood", Marguerite Laskares at Amazon.com.

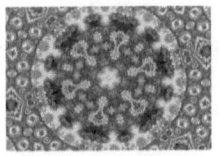

www.pacepublishing.com

Table of Contents

Frontispieces

About the Author	3
Other Books and Publications by the Author	4
Dedication	5
Acknowledgements	7
Prologue	13
Foreword	15
Epigraph	21
Introduction	23

Reflections

The Subconscious Song	27
Inspirational Background	29
Poem	33
Reader's Reflections	37
Listen!	43
Inspirational Background	45
Poem	49
Reader's Reflections	51
Beauty's New Day	57
Inspirational Background	59
Poem	63
Reader's Reflections	67
That's ENUF!!!	73
Inspirational Background	75
Poem	83
Song	85
Reader's Reflections	89
A Wavering Mind	95
Inspirational Background	97
Poem	99
Reader's Reflections	101

Emotions Are Powers	107
Inspirational Background	109
Poem	117
Reader's Reflections	125
"Techno" Indeed!	131
Inspirational Background	133
Poem	141
Reader's Reflections	151
Joy Unspeakable and Full of Glory	157
Inspirational Background	159
Poem	165
Reader's Reflections	169
Whatever Happened To "Me"?	175
Inspirational Background	177
Poem	181
Song	185
Reader's Reflections	191
Somewhere There's An Answer	197
Inspirational Background	199
Poem	203
Reader's Reflections	207
Preparing The REAL ME	213
Inspirational Background	215
Poem	219
Song	223
Reader's Reflections	227
Epilogue	233
Poem	235
Reader's Reflections	237
Reading List	243

Prologue

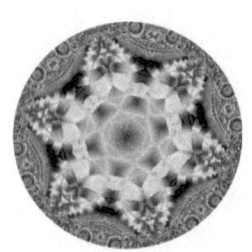

Dear Seeker of Those **"Deeper Things"**,

Come share
    A cup of tea with me,
        And feast upon
            Some poetry;

Prepare your space
    To sit a while,
        And hear the Music
            Of this style.

As you relax
    From all you do
        You'll find herein
            A **peace** that's true!

Perhaps a tear
    Will then break through,
        Or, perchance,
            A **laugh** or two!

So, whether you
    Are by yourself,
        With CD player
            On the shelf,

Or whether
    With your friends
        Who share
            Your love for air
                That's **really** rare!

Allow your hearts
    To take new wings,
        And ponder
            These **delicious** things!

                    Vanessa

Foreword

> *"**Kaleidoscope,** n. 1. an optical tube in which bits of glass and beads are shown in changing symmetrical forms by reflection in two or more mirrors as the tube is turned. 2. anything that shifts continually."*
> *The Random House Dictionary,*
> *Ballentine Books, New York*

> *"**Kaleidoscope** , ...; picturesquely diversified."*
> *The Practical Standard Dictionary*
> *of the English Language,*
> *Funk & Wagnalls Company,*
> *New York, 1928*

As a child I spent many enjoyable hours looking into my kaleidoscope, and being fascinated by the beauty and form of its ever-changing colorful designs.

"Kaleidoscope" is a beautiful word to describe the experience and purpose of this book, for We are each a precious jewel within the giant **Kaleidoscope** of Life!

Wikipedia.org adds another layer to our understanding of the word "**kaleidoscope**". It is made up of three Ancient Greek words: kalos, beautiful, beauty + eidos, that which is seen, form, shape + SCOPE, ... (skopeō), "to look to, to examine", hence, "observation of beautiful forms." **That's** the way I want to look at life!!!

We live in an exciting kaleidoscopic age of discovery (both personal and collective) and technological advancement, and the pruning of those two branches of our life's tree will determine the quality of the fruit that we bear. It has been my experience, and my observation, that, as wonderful as the technological world is, it may be costing us our Hu-man-ness!

We want to appreciate and know what wonders are out there in the technological world for us to use, but we also want to grow as Hu-mans to our fullest capacity. We are in the process of discovering the fullness of the awesome creatures that we ARE, and these advanced Beings will surely require advanced technologies to accomplish our potentials. But, the challenge we face is that We must be careful to maintain our Hu-man-ness as the King in Our Castle.

In my observation sometimes Hu-man-ness and technology are two magnets that are turned the wrong way, ..., repelling each other instead of empowering each other. As the advanced Beings that we are becoming, we must learn that, instead of using our intellectual powers to seek out and manage all the technologies offered to Us, we can allow our Hu-man-ness to **attract** only the technology that is useful to Us! We are daily bombarded with a veritable ocean of thoughts and tantalizing distractions that are calculated to cloud our minds and keep us from our individual and collective potentials. In the daily diet of time-wasting television, Internet and the other electronic media, and the myriad of books that have no relationship to the development of our virtuous character and callings, We often find our Hu-man-ness is overwhelmed. We "short out" because there is simply too much volume being pushed through our weakened filters for us to handle!

We Hu-mans have a basic need to pause, reflect, and connect to our real "Home" center. As the saying goes, "Come apart before you come apart"! We need to give ourselves time to awaken to our own possibilities!

This is a Poetry book. It is not a scientific dissertation. Poets want to provoke, educate, awaken, feel, think, inspire, and reflect, so that their personal awakenings will help to encourage a universal awakening. This book, and the ensuing Volumes, will continue to unfold reflections on the ongoing awakening experiences of our life's journey, in the hope that we will all grow together into the awesome Promises and Possibilities that We ARE!

As we turn the kaleidoscope of life we reflect upon the whole picture of past, present, and future experiences that make up the many facets of the diamond that we each are. Each "**Reflection**" in this book portrays a life's "**Meaningful Reflection**" and the many facets of revelation and growth presented by that life experience.

Wikipedia.com continues with its definition of "**kaleidoscope**": "A **Kaleidoscope** operates on the principle of multiple reflection, where several mirrors are placed at an angle to one another, ...". You see, in reality, we are each an important and colorful piece of the "picturesquely diversified" **kaleidoscope** of life!

Writing, singing, painting, building, gardening, etc., are all "tools" that we use to express the creative stirrings that are ever within ourselves. We are born creators, looking for a means of expression. Joy comes when we roll up our sleeves and give our creative stirrings actual form and beauty. Great satisfaction comes when we are able to fit our piece into the totality of the puzzle of creation!

I usually feel a poem coming on for a specific reason, ..., something that I am studying at the time, or some phrase that strikes me with deep meaning, or some "Aha!" moment when all of a sudden I understand an idea or concept at a deeper level than before.

*We are living in an exciting age of "Aha!" moments, so, as you turn the kaleidoscope of **your** life, I invite you to use the space provided in this book as a sounding-board for your own personal awakenings in your life, in your quest toward finding and fulfilling your life's purpose, and in the ever-deepening development of your rich spiritual walk.*

Welcome to my world!

www.pacepublishing.com

"cre-ate´, ..., 1. To cause to come into existence; especially, to produce out of nothing. 2. To produce as a new construction out of existing materials."

The Practical Standard Dictionary;
Funk & Wagnalls Company,
New York, 1928

Oh, I feel a poem coming on!!! ....

"cre-a´tion, ..., 1. The act of creating;
production without use of preexistent material;
...; 2. An act of construction,
physical or mental;
the combining or organizing
of existing materials
into new form; ...."

The Practical Standard Dictionary;
Funk & Wagnalls Company,
New York, 1928

Oh, I do, indeed, feel a poem coming on!!! ....

Introduction

Massive Creative Abilities lie in the hearts and minds of all of us, but sometimes these deep wells of self expression need a little priming before they will pump out the flowing waters of our creative energies! That is the purpose of these Volumes. I'm on a mission, and that mission is to awaken the sleeping genius in the heart of every person, one life at a time, and collectively, until we all know the joy of accomplishment, and until the focus of hu-man-ity is upon the creation of order and beauty in all forms.

Creativity is contagious! When we are around other "creators" our own creative juices start to flow, and we find ourselves swimming in that stream of energy that lights our own sparks of creativity. Like dead batteries that are suddenly hooked to jumper cables that are connected to the universe itself, we spring into an awakened state! Wow! We can't wait to put our new ideas into production!

It is exciting to me when an idea, or concept that I am studying, or a particularly strong emotional response to the myriad of life's experiences, or a just downright funny situation begins to formulate itself inside my mind as a poem! I'm learning to recognize it, ..., that funny sense of humor that lives somewhere inside of me, ..., that seems to understand what I am thinking about much better than I do, and begins to restate my ponderings in such rhyming words of clarity that I am sent scurrying for my pen and paper, lest I forget the tantalizing nuggets these Muses are offering.

It is the creative process at its best. It starts with the germ of a thought, and then it takes on its own identity as a poem. Then that poem needs to be couched in the story of its creation, and in a beautiful visual setting that enhances its message. And then, it must be given music and sound! We are sensory creatures, and we perceive our world through all of our senses. Let's awaken them all, and put them all to work in our quest for advancement!

We really need each other, and the encouragement that our associations bring. And so, I am sharing my thoughts, and poems, and music, and words with you in the hope that they will enhance your enjoyment of life, and prime the pump of your own creative genius! Space has been provided in this book at the end of every "**Reflection**" so that you can record your own "Reflections" and ideas, and creative musings. Everyone has a piece of this life's puzzle, and we need them all, YOURS AND MINE. The picture will not be complete until we have all contributed our part. Together we can fill our world with the order and beauty that we are all craving.

Oops! There it is! ...! WE are the ones that we have been waiting for all along to build the world of our dreams! Take your tools in hand, and let's begin!

www.pacepublishing.com

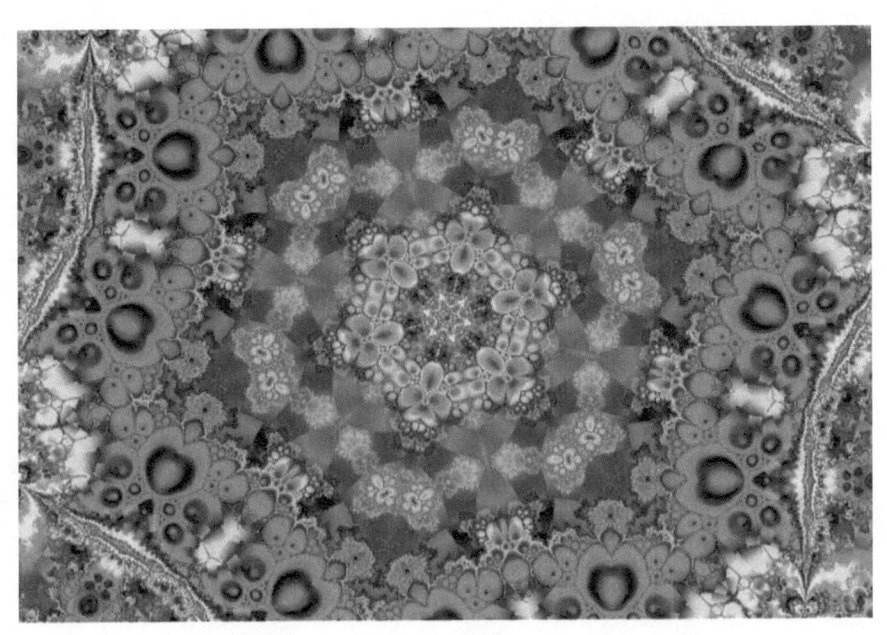

The Subconscious Song

www.pacepublishing.com

"The Subconscious Song"
Inspirational Background

We were producing our half-hour weekly television programs at the rate of about four programs per week, and the studio time was scheduled for the next day. I needed to be prepared to do at least two programs, but life had been a bit hectic that week. It seemed that there was no time for the creative process to germinate anything of the magnitude of a meaningful, musical, and visually beautiful half-hour television program. Normally, it would take twenty, or more, hours to envision and pull it all together.

I went about the business of patching all the holes that seemed to be in my bucket that week, but, Producer, Host, and Singer that I am, my subconscious antenna had always been up, searching for that "signal" that would bail the creative part of me out when the lights and cameras were turned on.

It was late in the evening, and I was quiet, and tired. ... But, ..., there it was, ..., that Still Small Voice; ...; And, ..., could it be, ..., when I had been seemingly too busy to listen ... ?

But, there it was!! ...!! I felt a poem coming on, ..., and it was about something that I **knew** to be true. Experience had shown me that there is almost always a song, from somewhere deep within my Soul, that would roll up inside me, if I would only "**Listen**", reach down deep enough to allow it expression, and give it Voice. It didn't come out of my conscious thinking. It seemed not to be touched by Hu-man hands; ...; just the free flow of "**The Subconscious Song**". The wonder of it all was that its message was timely, and that I felt so peaceful and satisfied after it was over. That feeling of being grounded, and "at One" with myself, and my world, left the very air around me pregnant with hope, possibility, and contentment.

And then, as if the Muses had opened the spout full wide, there came **another!** ...! Well, I needed **two** programs!

The guest that was scheduled for the next day's shoot "happened" to be my good friend, a pianist who is wonderfully gifted and trained in the art of improvisation. As a pipe organist, it was expected that she could improvise at the console of the mighty organ when certain parts of the church service took place. That invaluable experience came in handy that day.

"Quiet on the set, ..., Five, four, three, ...,". The magical atmosphere of the studio at "curtain time" came to life, and we were on. I opened the program, and read the first poem that I had received the night before. My friend and guest played an improvised accompaniment to my reading of "**The Subconscious Song**" poem. The very air within and without us was pregnant with a prophetic flow, ..., which lasted for the entire twenty-eight minutes of the program! After the written poem had finished, she continued to play music that had not been heard before, that enhanced, and elicited the spontaneous poetry that flowed unhindered and unbroken from The Great Poet Who lives within Me! It was one of those exhilarating moments under the lights!

Naturally, We called that program "**The Subconscious Song**", for, indeed, that is what flowed forth then, and will again, any time we put our antennas up, and allow the Song within us to take form!

We did, indeed, feel a poem coming on that day!

www.pacepublishing.com

Poem
The Subconscious Song

GOD is **TRYING**
    To get through,
        To tell you
            What He says **to you**;
            To SING **to you**
                Of the things
                  He's said,
                      And give you
                          Your **OWN**
                              Daily bread.

For, often
    He has tried to say,
        Some wondrous **TRUTH**
            To bring your way,
                But found that **you**
                      Were bound to sing
                          Some **lower** than
                              Eternal thing.

So, ...,
 Set your thoughts
  On things above,
   And **KNOW**
    There is a God
     That's **LOVE,**
      Who wants to share
       HIS thoughts with you,
        And **LEAD**
         In all you say
          And do.

It really is
 An awesome thing
  To think that **GOD**
   Would really **SING!** ...!
    The even **MORE**
     Amazing part
      Is that We
       Can **HEAR** Him
        OUR HEART!

So, ...,
 When that Song
  Begins to roll
   From somewhere deep
    Within your soul,
     Just pause,
      And let the message ring,
       And **KNOW**
        That He Who sings
         Is **KING!**

The **AWESOME**
 And **ETERNAL ONE,**
  Who was,
   And is,
    And is to come; ...;
     Who runs the Universe,
      Its true;
       But, still,
        He has **a Song**
         For You!

The One Who sang,

    "Let there be light.",

        Now sings a **NEW SONG**

            With His Might;

                But this time

                    Only **YOU** can hear

                      His **Voice** ring

                        In **your**

                            Inner ear!

So, now,

    All that's left to do

        Is **TAKE**

            What He has said to you;

                Receive His comfort!

                    Hear His Word!

                      Then go and **DO**

                      The things

                        You've heard.

Vanessa Conaway Pace
Seattle, Washington, October 2, 1998

The Subconscious Song

This Is Your
Invitation
To Create!

Dear Seeker of Those "Deeper Things",

Now "**Listen**".
    Hear that Song
        Inside?
            Just take
                A moment
                    To abide,

And "hear"
    The song
        YOUR Soul
           Does Sing, ...,
                No need
                    To "think hard",
                        Or to "plan"
                            Anything;

Be sure
    That YOU write it
        As it comes,
           And share it
                With a world
                    That "Hums"!

Now Its YOUR Turn To Be "Creator"!
Put YOUR Thoughts Here, and Read Them Later!

*Now Its YOUR Turn To Be "Creator"!
Put YOUR Thoughts Here, and Read Them Later!*

Now Its YOUR Turn To Be "Creator"!
Put YOUR Thoughts Here, and Read Them Later!

*Now Its YOUR Turn To Be "Creator"!
Put YOUR Thoughts Here, and Read Them Later!*

Listen!

www.pacepublishing.com

"Listen!"
Inspirational Background

Well, I **had** asked for help in producing **two** programs in the television studio that day, ..., and, ..., I **had** received **two** poems late in the evening before, ..., and, ..., the creative juices **were** still flowing after we finished the first "improvisational" program.

So, we rolled cameras again. And, I opened the second program, ..., and then read the **second** poem, accompanied by my friend's inspired improvisational accompaniment.

Can lightning strike twice? **Yes!** Indeed it can! After the reading of the second poem that I had been given the night before the shoot, we continued in the same spontaneous poetic manner for the remainder of the **second** twenty-eight minute program, thus proving, ...,

When we really
    Need some answers
        All we have to to
            Is "**Listen**"

To the Little Voice
    That speaks inside
        With little gems
            That glisten;

But, sometimes
    We're much too busy
        With our own
            Well thought out Plans
            To consider that
                The Voice inside
                    Is higher up
                        Than man's.

We make
    An awful racket
        With our never ending chatter,
        So We can't hear
            The Truth
                About the things
                    That really matter.

And the thought
> That We
>> Are cared about
>>> By Someone
>>>> Who's unseen
>>>>> In a shallow-thinking Era
>>>>>> Borders closely
>>>>>>> On obscene!

But The Truth
> That has been sung out
>> In the songs
>>> Down through the ages
>>>> Bears the message
>>>>> That the **Listeners**
>>>>>> Become
>>>>>>> Our real life
>>>>>>>> **Sages,**

Who bring Wisdom
> To the Seekers
>> Who will take
>>> The time to "**Listen**"

And give them Plans
*That they can **do**,*
And even get
To christen!

*Oh, **yes!** Definitely, ..., there is a poem coming on!!!*

Poem
Listen!

"*Listen*!" God is speaking!
    HEAR HIS Voice;
        The message that comes
            Is of HIS OWN choice!

Specially coded
    So you can receive
        The answers you need
            If you'll only BELIEVE!

The Word He is sending
    Is special for YOU!
        It's carefully tailored
            To carry you through!

It's perfectly crafted
    With the REAL YOU in mind
        By The Father Who made you
            Who's gentle and kind.

He knows **HOW** to call you,
>But sometimes the line's **busy**
>>When you've gone off ALONE
>>>And **your life's in a tizzy!**

But Father Knows Best,
>And will patiently wait
>>For the time when you're **QUIET**
>>>To set your life straight.

His **Voice** has been speaking, ...,
>**Deep** calling to **Deep**, ...,
>>He wanted to help you,
>>>But you were asleep.

So, **find time to LISTEN.**
>HIS **VOICE** is within.
>>He's waiting with answers.
>>>**How long has it been?**

Vanessa Conaway Pace
Seattle, Washington, October 2, 1998

Listen!

This Is Your Invitation To Create!

Dear Seeker of Those "Deeper Things",

Some practice
    In writing
        Will waken
            Your gift,
                And YOU"LL
                    Even find
                        That YOUR Spirit
                            Will lift

As YOU "**Listen!**"
    For messages
        Sent YOU
            From "Home";
            And then,
                Write them all down, ...,
                    Soon YOU"LL have
                      Your own
                            "Tome"!!!

Now Its YOUR Turn To Be "Creator"!
Put YOUR Thoughts Here, and Read Them Later!

*Now Its YOUR Turn To Be "Creator"!
Put YOUR Thoughts Here, and Read Them Later!*

Now Its YOUR Turn To Be "Creator"!
Put YOUR Thoughts Here, and Read Them Later!

*Now Its YOUR Turn To Be "Creator"!
Put YOUR Thoughts Here, and Read Them Later!*

Beauty's New Day

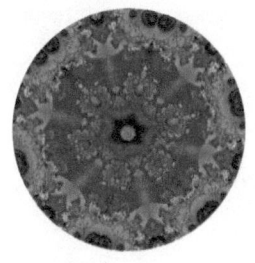

www.pacepublishing.com

"Beauty's New Day"
Inspirational Background

*I*t was all too much for me to encompass. I was a pretty "normal" person, with a pretty "normal" world view. I had been raised as an earthbound farm girl—the stars, Moon, and Sun were "up there", and **we** were "down here". And, of course, we were the **only** ones in the whole "universe"! I didn't even **know** that word at that time. Not consciously. I could spell it, and read it, but, the **reality** of it was way outside of my corn patch.

Even went I spent all those years (should I have said, "squandered"?) in univers-ities, it was totally outside my thinking that there could be "life" anywhere other than on Divinely chosen Planet Earth!

But what is **this?**! I was surfing the Internet late one night, chasing down rabbit trails, as one often does with this technological wonder that opens worlds to us, and somehow stumbled on the United Nations website. Never been there before, so I started poking around, mindlessly clicking different buttons to see what they would open up.

Then "life", ..., **my life**, ..., forever changed. I had "stumbled" into the "Galactic Treaties" section of the United Nations website!

DISCONNECT! OVERLOAD!

Everything went blank for me. It was as if the whole world stopped and blanked out to me. My mind simply could not process the implications of that phrase fast enough, so I couldn't even think. Gradually the whirring stopped in my brain, and pieces of information began to click together.

Why did **we**, the obviously (to me) only inhabitants of all of space, need a "Galactic Treaties" department within the United Nations, ..., unless we were actively communicating with..., ..., ..., No! ...! No! ...! There **can't** be "others" "out there"!

And, if there are "others" "out there", and someone is making "Treaties" with "them", then "they" must be coming **here** (since I couldn't **imagine** that we would, or could, be going **there**), and talking (doing business?) (making war?) with someone **here** who KNOWS that "they" are REAL!

PROCESSING!!! PROCESSING!!!

OVERLOAD!!!   OVERLOAD!!!
"ALL CIRCUITS ARE CURRENTLY BUSY"!!!

I was trying to process this whole thing, but a lifetime of programming doesn't totally dissolve in an instant. However, the foundations **were** badly cracked!

I had already learned that there are "rivers" in space, so that caused me to wonder, "Is that what they meant in the old song, "Shall We Gather At The River?"!

Oh! I **definitely** hear a poem coming on! ...! ...!

www.pacepublishing.com

Poem
Beauty's New Day!

She kept her word
    In the cold of the day;
        And she came to brush
            All the clouds away.

For her name was **"Beauty"**
    And her Style was **Grace**;
        And she showed great Love
            By the smile on her Face.

For the Time has come
    In the scheme of things
        When the people will **know**
            As the Earth-bell rings;

That **a new day** has blessed us,
    And the Time has arrived
        When the **Folks** shall arrive
            From the **Other Side!!**

There'll be **Singing** and **Laughter**
    As **The Family** comes,
        And knows once again
           Those from the **Other** homes!

When we all were together
    On that Glorious Side,
        Making **Plans** for our time
           In the **Hu-man/Earth-tide**.

For we heard the call clearly,
    And we **knew** from that place
        That we'd sacrifice dearly
           When we landed from Space.

But, with Great Love we've chosen
    To be here at this time
        To be part of the closin'
           Of this moment in time.

Yes, we **wanted** to be
    In **this moment of Grace**,
        In this **Octave**, to **rise**
           With the rest of our Race!

And to pull others UP,
> And the "things" along, too,
>> That have withered, and paled, ...,
>>> Let them all become New!

For **a New Day has dawned**
> That is No longer cloudy,
>> And **we're finally Home;**
>>> **Let the Party get ROUDY!!!**

Let us celebrate Light,
> **And the Love that we've cherished.**
>> **For the Future is Bright! ...!**
>>> **Not a Particle perished!!!!**

Vanessa Conaway Pace
Seattle, Washington, January 6, 2005

www.pacepublishing.com

Beauty's New Day!

***This Is* Your
Invitation
To Create!**

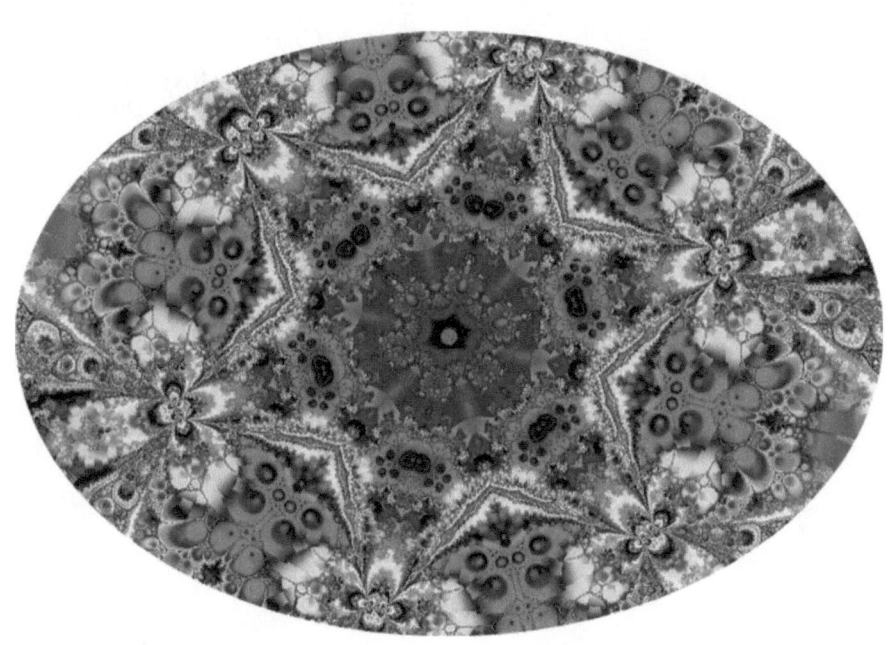

Dear Seeker of Those "Deeper Things",

Keep YOUR Mind
    On alert,
        And YOUR pen
            At the ready, ...,
                Soon those new thoughts
                    Will come
                        In a stream
                            That is steady.

Just remember
    To write
        Them all down
            In a jiffy,
                And soon
                    YOU"LL be
                        Creating poems
                        That are
                            "Spiffy"!

Now Its YOUR Turn To Be "Creator"!
Put YOUR Thoughts Here, and Read Them Later!

Now Its YOUR Turn To Be "Creator"!
Put YOUR Thoughts Here, and Read Them Later!

*Now Its YOUR Turn To Be "Creator"!
Put YOUR Thoughts Here, and Read Them Later!*

Now Its YOUR Turn To Be "Creator"!
Put YOUR Thoughts Here, and Read Them Later!

That's ENUF!!!

www.pacepublishing.com

"That's ENUF!!!"
Inspirational Background

$\mathcal{M}$y head was reeling again. It seems to be a constant condition these days! This process of "awakening" from Humanity's eons of slumber is painful; ...; at least to those of us who thought we had learned a fair amount, and therefore had it all figured out.

I had put my eight years in at univers-ities. And, I had done the years of music study and voice training. And, I had diligently studied and served my twenty-five years in the church. And, I had dutifully spent that same twenty-five years showing up, and giving an honest day's work for what they called an honest day's pay in Big Business. That was what we had been told to do in order to have a successful life—study and prepare, develop your unique gifts and talents, work hard, and the world will beat a path to your door looking for your expertises—and, I was working hard, with every ounce of strength that was in me, to follow The Plan for Success that had been taught us.

But, something was wrong. "Success", promised prosperity, joy, fulfillment, and peace seemed to elude me. And questions crowded themselves into my mind. .... And, it was happening all too regularly.

I was blessed to have practical-minded parents who insisted that I understand both the cause and the effect of my actions. They helped me gather facts before making a decision, and taught to me to live by their admonition to "Ask questions. Ask **lots** of questions. And don't rest until you are satisfied that the answers make some sense to you." They helped me to reason things out, and come to logical conclusions based on the facts that had been gathered, and not simply on the emotion of the moment.

But it was becoming more and more obvious to me that things in life (both mine, and the collective) weren't coming to "logical conclusions". It seemed that events in our world were not coming to decent and logical conclusions, even though we touted the "advanced" state of our society. Why wasn't I, and "society", deliriously happy, successful, and prosperous? We **seemed** to have all the right "tools". ....

*I **believed*** *that I had discovered "Truth", and was attempting to walk in it, ..., and yet, why so many inconsistencies? So, I got real brave one day and glibly blurted to out to The Spirit, "Just show me **The Truth**. I don't care what it costs me, just show me **The Truth**."*

Well, I suggest that you not do that, ..., not unless you are ready to have your whole world turned upside down!

*But, maybe we **need** to have our worlds (as we have passively allowed them to happen) reshaped, and re-molded into something that more closely resembles **The Truth**. And, yes, **The Truth** is **The Truth**, and is applicable to everybody. There are no "special" circumstances that allow certain "special" people to break the Laws by which the universe operates! The very word "law" indicates that it is something that works every time! We may as well get used to it, and learn to live by them, and cooperate with them, because universal law, and our response to it, is inexorably shaping our lives and destinies! The **applications** of universal principle may vary, but gravity works for everybody—unless you know the higher law that* allows you to transcend it! My gut feelings were telling me that maybe things really aren't what we have been led to believe.

I remembered the day that I bought a little red book at a church bazaar back in Boston. There was no title anywhere on the cover, but for some reason I **had** to have that book. So, I spent my last few pennies for that one, and a book called "The Wump World" for my young children.

We snuggled in on that beautiful fall Sunday afternoon in New England, and I read the children the story of the "Wumps".

As I remember the story, the "Wumps" were a people who lived happily on a beautiful imaginary planet, ..., until they were taken over by a group that wanted to control their lives and to profit from their labors. That group covered the "Wumps'" beautiful planet with pollution, and cement, and the destructions of wars; and then, when the planet was no longer livable, they blasted themselves off the of that devastated planet, bound for greener fields for themselves, and another weaker and sleeping society to destroy. The "Wumps" hid underground for protection during their captors' wars, and when that group left, the "Wumps" came up out of the caves of their captivity to view the damages. They were left with the daunting task of cleanup and recovery of their once beautiful planet. My apologies to the author if I have misunderstood or forgotten some of the story. ("The Wump World": Bill Peet, Houghton Mifflin Co., Boston, 1970)

That was the ***first*** "message" to me that day.

After the children were properly fed, bathed, bedded down, and sung to sleep, I pulled out the little red book and cozied myself in for a wonderful evening of reading.

It wasn't long before I got the shock of my life. **No! That simply could *not* be!** The earth-shattering message in the little red book told me that there were despicable people in the world, that I had been taught to respect and honor, who were actually **creating** wars for their own profit!!! **No! That could not be!** We fought wars because someone was threatening us. Or, because someone was oppressing someone who was too weak to defend themselves. Then, of course, we, being mighty, would show ourselves as the conquering heroes. **Nobody** would send other people's children into battle for their own profit! **No one** would play both sides of a war in order to profit from the sale of munitions! We were a "principled" people, who fought for "the right"! ...! But, there it was,..., in black on white, ..., evidence that was hard to deny.

I walked the paths along the Charles River for days, numb, grieving, and incredulous. **No!** That could not be! **No one** would harm, and even send other people's children and loved ones into harm's way for their own profit. I was brought up with an idealistic view of the world, believing that everyone was pulling together and working for the common good. That's the way it was on our farm.

We lived in the country, and our house was separated from the other houses in our farming community by large areas of greenbelt and farmland. We, like the others around us, were a bit isolated from the neighbors, and therefore, we had to be (and **wanted** to be) self-sufficient. We all **had** to work together to ensure that we would have sufficient food, clothing, and shelter. We **depended** on each other, and, we **trusted** that everyone was working toward the common good.

As a little girl growing up in that environment I had a sense of trust built into me. I was brought up to honor those in "leadership", ..., in a world that taught that it was honorable to fight for your own rights (as long as you did it respectfully, and no one was hurt), and to defend the rights of weaker ones by reason and debate—**never** by violence.

Now, this little red book was telling me that multitudes of wonderful people are being exploited by a few individuals whose mindset has been misguided. That idea was taking some processing, and my old idealism was, of necessity (when facing the facts), dying.

But we are an indomitable lot! The Hu-man spirit will not be snuffed out, and it won't even be held down for long periods of time. Something in us rises up and says, "**No! We won't be enslaved, and those who endeavor to enslave us shall be removed.**" Something in our Hu-man soul reminds us that we are not alone, that there's a part of our family that remained on those distant shores that we left to come here, and that they are faithful to us and to the projects we all agreed upon before we left those shores and became the "boots on the ground" ambassadors that we are!

Oh **yes**, indeed, we are, at our very core, free, and we have within us everything that we need to accomplish everything that we came here to do.

Now I **definitely** hear a poem coming on! But, ..., wait! It has a **melody**! In the words of the old song, "I feel a song coming on, ...,"!

Poem
That's ENUF!!!

Oh, The people have decided "**That's ENUF!!!**"
    For we know that we won't put up with this stuff.
        We've been ripped off, raped, and gutted
            By a pow'r that has been strutted;
                Now we're gonna bring
                      Our Planet back to snuff!!

We've been pulled apart and mangled, that is true.
    But that doesn't mean we don't **know** what to do.
        There's an enemy that's plotted.
            O, but now their plot has rotted;
                And they're slinking
                      Toward a distant
                          Cosmic zoo!

We've been told that we must "listen and obey".
    But we won't believe the empty words they say.
        They've been dumbed down, too! ...,
        ..., Its certain!
            And right now they're really hurtin';
                'Cause the game is up,
                      And we'll no longer play!

What they thought that they'd created is a farce!
> For we now know that they've landed here from Mars!
>> Well, they can't stop what **we've** come for;
>>> And their game is really done for;
>>>> 'Cause we're gettin' help
>>>>> From way beyond the stars!

Yes! We're welcoming the help that's coming through.
> For without them we would not know what to do.
>> We **are** mighty, and we're learnin'
>>> But that fear was really churnin'
>>>> That we'd end up in
>>>>> A Universal stew!

So, the good news is that we can be in peace;
> And can grant our anxious souls that sweet release;
>> For our Family's come to get us;
>>> And their added strength will let us
>>>> Freely **BE**, and **DO**,
>>>>> All things that
>>>>>> We would please!!!!!

Vanessa Conaway Pace
Seattle, Washington, May 21, 2005

Song

That's ENUF!!!

Vanessa Conaway Pace   Vanessa Conaway Pace

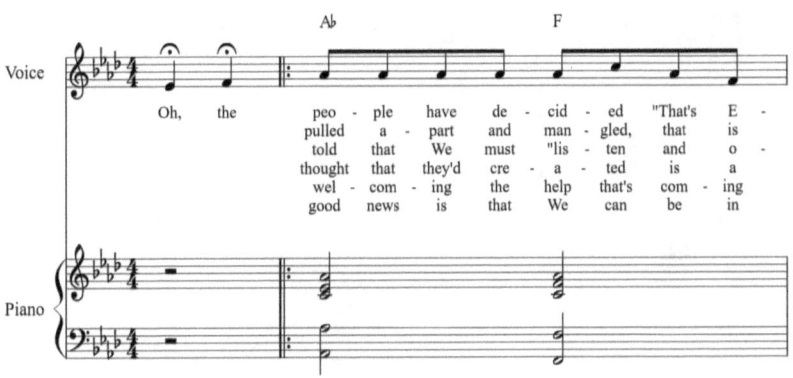

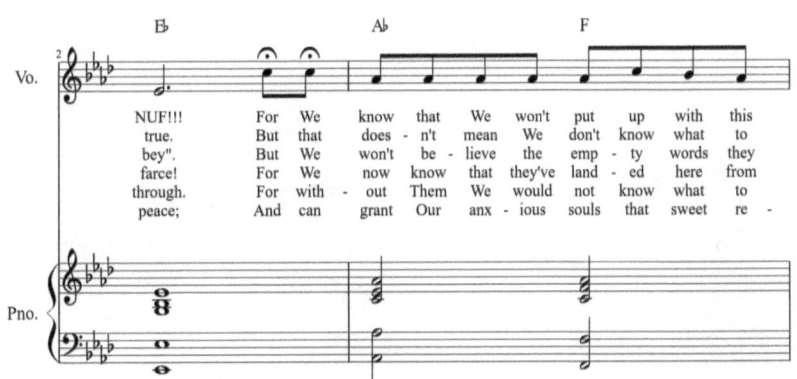

2005

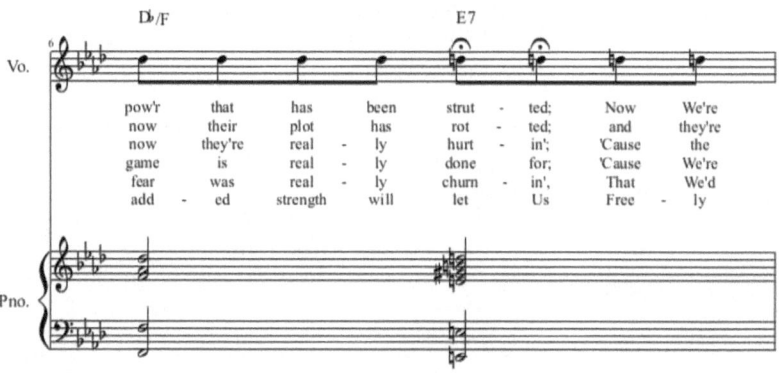

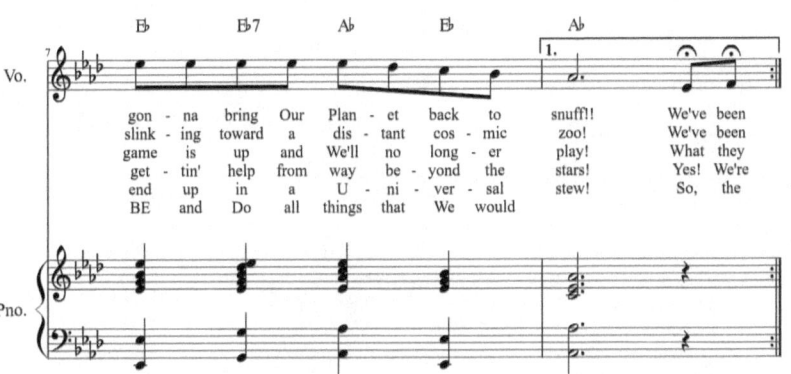

www.pacepublishing.com

That's ENUF!!!

This Is Your Invitation To Create!

Dear Seeker of Those "Deeper Things",

In these days
    When We're all
        Waking up
            To new Truths,
                We're not looking
                    For any more
                        Fictions
                            Or spoofs!

But, the new
    Revelations
        Are coming
            Much faster,
                And, if We
                    Don't record them,
                        It could mean
                            Disaster!

So, Quick!
    Write it down
        When a new thought's
            Discovered,
                Then share
                    With the others
                        The Truths You've
                            Uncovered!!

Now Its YOUR Turn To Be "Creator"!
Put YOUR Thoughts Here, and Read Them Later!

Now Its YOUR Turn To Be "Creator"!
Put YOUR Thoughts Here, and Read Them Later!

Now Its YOUR Turn To Be "Creator"!
Put YOUR Thoughts Here, and Read Them Later!

Now Its YOUR Turn To Be "Creator"!
Put YOUR Thoughts Here, and Read Them Later!

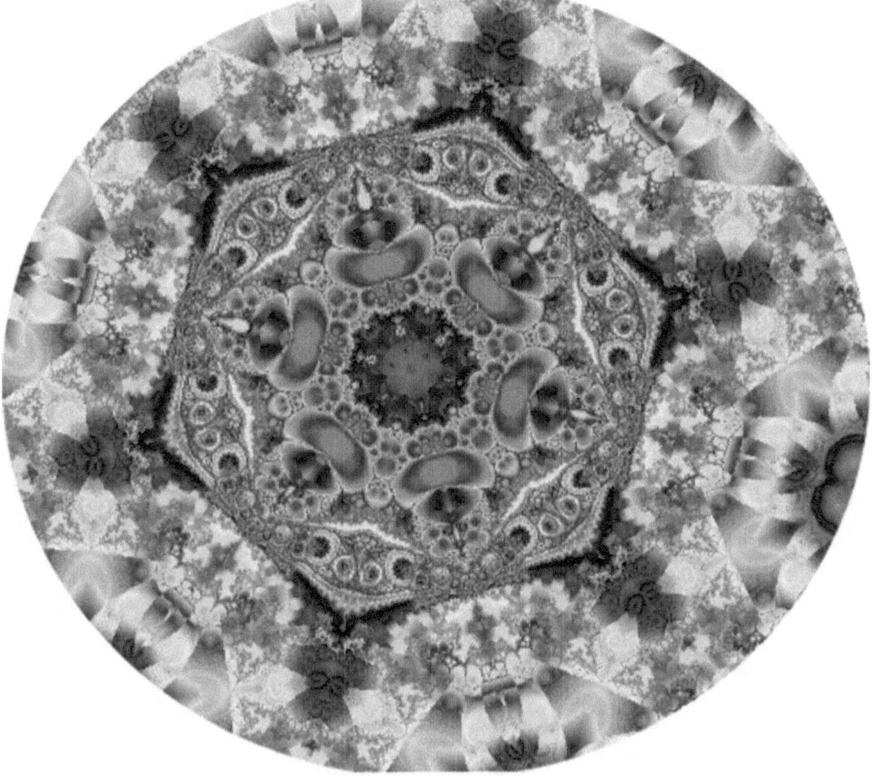

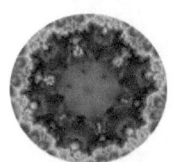

A Wavering Mind

(The International Library of Poetry, Editor's Choice Award, 1999)

www.pacepublishing.com

"A Wavering Mind"
Inspirational Background

It was the Summer of 1998, and the media was in full bloom. "Smut and Scandal" seemed to be deliciously on their minds, and had been the daily diatribe for much too long. The idea that "Love covers a multitude of sins," had long been trampled into the dirt, and the people—at least **THIS** "people"--had grown very weary of months of being fed the same old worn-out diet of propaganda cloaked as "news". Our souls longed to be able to turn on televisions or radios and hear something **UPLIFTING**, ..., something that would speak of "**goodness**", or that would herald the "**creativity**" of one of our nation's valued inhabitants, ..., or would sing the praises of one who had **accomplished something wonderful** that would be for the good of all, ..., or, even to be able to relax to the strains of beautiful music wafting through our airwaves, or to revel in scenes of beauty and majesty being broadcast through our airspace.

The innate, wondrously created Being that we are longs for fellowship with Truth, Beauty, and The Light. The more we become aware of who we really are, and from whence we have come, the more we shudder at darkness, and run to that which manifests Glory!

    Deep within the Genuine Real Being that we **are** there is a bona fide "**rebel**" that **will** stand up on its hind legs when our senses are offended, or the peace that we have created in our own world is defiled, or the clean "table" that has been prepared before us in the presence of our enemies is dumped upon, or, even when our considerable intelligence is openly scoffed at and dishonored, and say, "**No!!!** I won't take it anymore. I don't hafta, and I AIN'T GONNA!!! I can CHOOSE what I want to be, and I can CHOOSE what I want to hear, and I can CHOOSE what I want to think about."

    Ooops!!! There it is again!!!. I feel a poem coming on!

...

Poem
A Wavering Mind

The sun shall rise,
    And the sun shall set,
        But they just ain't
            Seen nothin' **yet**!

For **My Voice** shall be heard
    When **My Arm** shall shine,
        For there is no peace
            When the others entwine.

When they shuffle this way
    And they hem and haw that
        You hardly can tell
            Just **where** they're at!

But haven't **I** said
    For you to bear in mind
        Not to dabble
            With one of the **shifty kind?**

For they'll wiggle this way,
    And they'll squiggle toward that,
        And they'll want you to think
            That **they're** the diplomat.

But woe to the ones
    Who have been so blind
        As to follow the ways
            Of "**A Wavering Mind**".

                              Vanessa Conaway Pace
                    Seattle, Washington, The Summer of 1998

A Wavering Mind

This Is Your
Invitation
To Create!

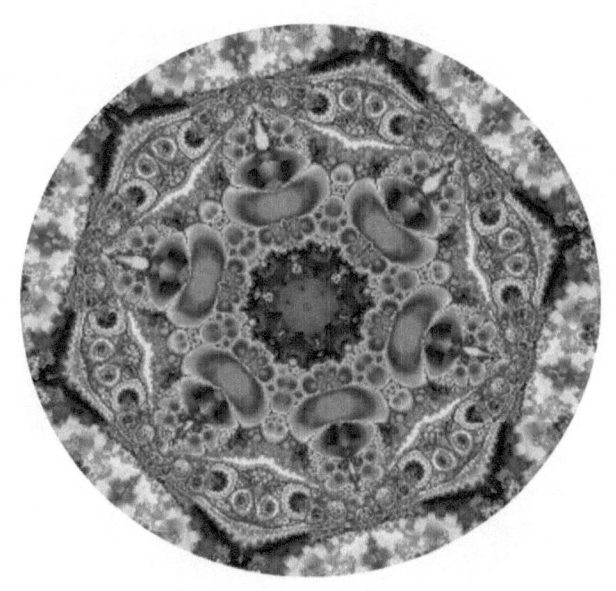

Dear Seeker of Those "Deeper Things",

I'm sure **You've**
    Had thoughts
        Of what's
            Bugging **You**,
                So, write them
                    All down
                        In a line
                            Or two,

And join in
    The party
        Of Creative Beings
            To express
                In YOUR words
                    All the dreams
                        Of YOUR "seeings"!

Just write
    What YOU "hear",
        And Sing
            Your own song,
                And soon
                    The whole world
                        Will be
                            Singing along!!

Now Its YOUR Turn To Be "Creator"!
Put YOUR Thoughts Here, and Read Them Later!

Now Its YOUR Turn To Be "Creator"!
Put YOUR Thoughts Here, and Read Them Later!

Now Its YOUR Turn To Be "Creator"!
Put YOUR Thoughts Here, and Read Them Later!

*Now Its YOUR Turn To Be "Creator"!
Put YOUR Thoughts Here, and Read Them Later!*

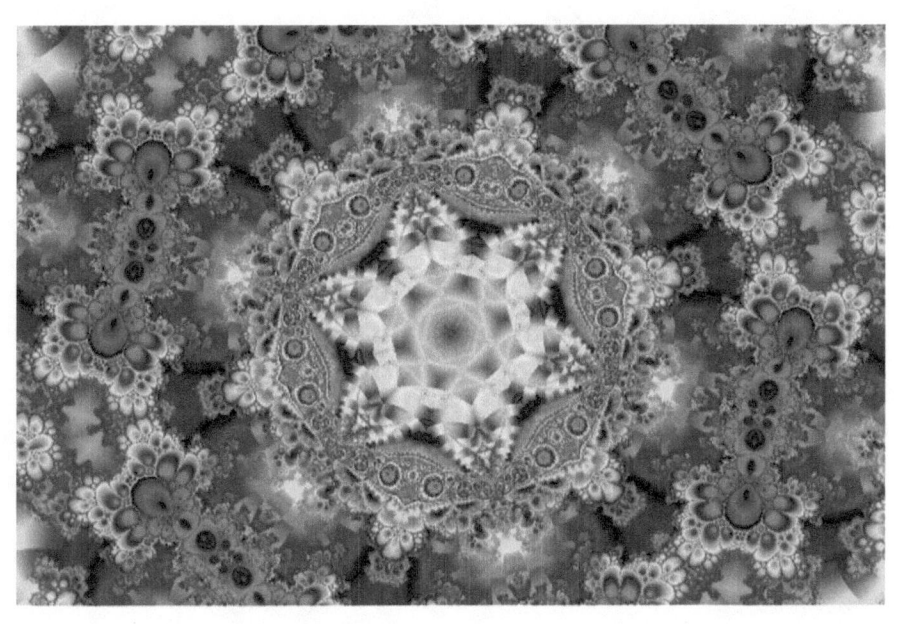

Emotions Are Powers!!!

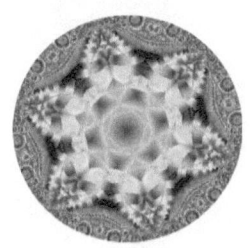

www.pacepublishing.com

"Emotions Are Powers!!!"
Inspirational Background

"*L*ife", at least my perception of it, was about to change, ..., ***again!***

My friends had just suggested a book to me that they were reading, and I could tell from the excitement in their voices it was changing their lives. Every once in a while a game-changing book is released into our planet (These "books" that keep "appearing" in my life are costing me a lot of sleep!), and those who have ears to hear are richer for this wonderful revelation from "Home". David R. Hawkins, M.D., PhD, had released such a book. At least to me, and to those who had recommended it to me, and to many others that I have since recommended the book to, this was a revelation that seemed at once new, and as comfortable as an old shoe. Something inside me gravitated to its message. It had a ring of truth to it that I immediately comprehended and embraced.

I remember a heated discussion with my Junior High School science teacher, who told us seventh grade know-it-alls that everything **vibrates**. I knew that he was wrong, and confidently declared him to be so! Everybody knows that rocks don't **move**! (Well, I was pretty sure they didn't move on our farm, unless we moved them!) They just sit there and do nothing! That was a mistake on my part! Our Science Teacher proceeded to offer scientific evidence that rocks do, indeed, **vibrate**! Wow!! It may be at a very slow rate that rocks vibrate, but I've since found that they DO actually **vibrate**! They **have** to vibrate, because every**thing** vibrates, and rocks are a "**thing**"!

As my mind has begun to wake up to the exciting reality of how things really work, I have since done more research into this "vibration" thing, and find it to be an amply proven fact! Everything vibrates.

When the different religious writings of the world try to describe how things were created we find statements such as, "In the beginning was the word" (The Bible, John 1:1), ..., **"sound"**, which, logically, is **vibration;** and, of course, the primal word of Indian Spirituality (and music), "..., Nada Brahma, means not only: God, the Creator, is sound; but also, (and above all): Creation, the cosmos, the world, is sound. And: Sound is the world." ("Nada Brahma:

The World Is Sound: Music and The Landscape of Consciousness": Joachim-Ernst Berendt, Destiny Books, Rochester, VT 05767, 1983) The Ancients seemed to clearly understand that vibration organizes Creation, and holds it together! Maybe we are going to have to rewrite the old song that declares, "Love makes the world go round". Somehow, singing "Vi-bra-tion makes the world go round" just doesn't have the same "ring" to it! Calling all Composers: As Awakening Hu-manity, We need new music written that sings out the Truths of Creation!!!

And, we now know that everything vibrates at its own unique rate, and that rate actually **determines** what that "thing" will be. In "Power vs. Force" Dr. David R. Hawkins had gone so far as to give exact numbers of the vibrational rates of things such as emotions, dis-eases, and even accidents! ("Power vs. Force, The Hidden Determinants of Human Behavior: An Anatomy of Consciousness"; Veritas Publishing, Post Office Box 3516 West Sedona, AZ 86340, Email: info@veritaspub.com)

For example, when we are in a room where someone is putting out a certain emotion (joy, anger, sorrow, etc.) the vibrations they put out can affect everyone in the room. We can **feel** the energy of their sadness, joy, etc. Based on twenty years of research, Dr. Hawkins has presented a "Map of Consciousness" showing the calibrated numerical rates of vibration for each of these attitudes and emotions.

It was fascinating to me to see a scientist be able to measure the elusive emotion of Love, and to be able to state that **Love** is the highest frequency, and, conversely, hate, and its companions, all register at much lower frequencies.

I liked that because it indicated an order of things. Each thought, each emotion, each action, and every **thing** seemed to have its own unique rate of vibration, and therefore, it would logically fit into a mathematical spectrum, and could be easily identified.

Dr. Masaru Emoto, groundbreaking researcher and world renowned author of many cutting-edge books on the true power of water from the perspective of science, healing, and mysticism ("The Healing Power of Water", Hay House, Inc., www.hayhouse.com), demonstrated this principle conclusively in a wonderful lecture that I attended. He held one tuning fork on one side of the stage, and his wife held another tuning fork of exactly the same pitch on the other side of the stage. When he struck his tuning fork, her tuning fork sprang into sympathetic vibration. If the frequency of her tuning fork had been even one vibrational number different from his it would not have responded! Since all truth is parallel, then I believe that We are the same way! We respond vibrationally to the emotional "tuning forks" of others.

Why is this important for all of us to understand? Because **"Emotions Are Powers"**, and, our destinies depend upon our receiving, understanding, knowing, and living in sync with these Divine Universal Principles.

Yes! I believe that the application of these universal Truths will drastically affect our future! Swimming upstream against the mighty current of universal law is probably beyond our puny capabilities! We'd be smarter to busy ourselves finding out how "The System" really works, and then implementing that life-giving knowledge in every area of our lives with all speed. We've all learned that spitting in the wind is not profitable, so now we are looking for a better way! And Dr. David R. Hawkins, Dr. Masaru Emoto, and many others of their courage, faithfulness to their chosen work, and brilliance, were showing me that there is indeed an all pervading "System" by which the universe operates, and, if We will operate Our lives in sync with its principles, We will find Ourselves living happy, successful, healthful, and prosperous lives in the wonderful world that We subconsciously crave, and know is possible!

Now, if "Power vs. Force" was and is correct (and I'm finding many others, both Ancient and modern, that agree with David Hawkins' analysis), then his listing of the frequencies of emotions shows us an important fact: Emotions are scientifically measurable, are creative powers in and of themselves, and they affect the frequency levels in and around us, thus changing our lives and our world. Knowing that should probably cause us to **think** before we allow an emotional tirade to pull us into a frequency lower than the Love frequency, which would consequently pull our lives and our world down into a less than desirable frequency level. We don't want to go there!

We've been somewhat aware of these different frequency levels (pitch goes up—faster vibes, and pitch goes down—slower vibes), but, since we really didn't understand them, or, worse yet, their effect on us, we basically just *ignored them, and thought on other things. There's always sports, or the evening news to distract us.*

*But, perhaps our subconscious awareness of universal principles has been trying to work its way through our acquired fog for a long time. We admonish ourselves to "rise above" the circumstances and situations in which we find ourselves, but I never really understood what that meant. That thought urges me that somehow I must pull myself up by my bootstraps, but how? How do I "rise above" my circumstances? Do I somehow fly off into the sky, and thus escape the consequences of my actions? We long ago made a joke of that idea by laughingly declaring, "It's hard to soar with eagles when you have to work with turkeys"! But we really didn't understand how to alter our altitude, …. At least **I** didn't.*

*Now David Hawkins was giving us a clue. If we could learn to **manage** our emotions, and change our thinking, we could spend more time in the higher virtues, instead of groveling in the lower altitudes of the Seven Deadly Sins, which, by the way, happen to include anger, envy, and all those other emotions that David Hawkins' research discovered broadcast a lower frequency. (I* personally liked Gandhi's own list of Seven Deadly Sins: "Wealth without Work; Pleasure without Conscience; Science without Humanity; Knowledge without Character; Politics without Principle; Commerce without Morality; and Worship without Sacrifice". Makes sense to me!)

The keys are in our hands! The methods are well known and easily understood. **The problem comes in when we realize that we must learn to manage our own emotions so that we put out and retain the energetic force of them, and learn to channel it in the direction of those things which we desire to accomplish!**

The real problem is that once We become aware of these Truths, We must also figure out "how shall We then live", and actually **do** something with the knowledge that we have gained. Education without action stuffs our shirts with a lot of thin air!

Yes! Hope is in the air! We are no longer victims! We can change our destiny!

Oh yes, ..., I do hear a poem coming on!

Poem
Emotions Are Powers!!!

Your **Emotions** are **Powers**
    That rise up within,
        That you've heard,
            Left "unbridled",
                Will lead you
                    To "sin".

But there's **One Little Truth**
    They've forgotten to say:
        Those **Emotions**
            Have **Value**, ...,
                Like a **CROP**,
                    Let us say,

That is coveted dearly
    By those who would Rule,
        For there's nothing
            That's left
                In **their** Energy Pool.

So they rape all your **Feelings,**
    And play your **Emotions,**
        To drain off
            Your Power
                To thicken
                    Their Potions.

For **Emotions** make **Energy**
    That produces a **"Tone"**, ...,
        A **Vibration,** ...,
            A Thought
                Sounding deep in our bone.

And that **Energy's sought**
    By the Creatures of Night,
        For without
            High **Emotion**
                They can't produce **Light!**

For the **Energy** needed
    To make a Light bright
        On the scale
            Of our Mind
                Is just Way out of sight!

But our **Emotions** can soar
    To loftier heights,
        And can
            Generate **POWER**
                That can turn on
                    Those **Lights**!!

For each Thought, ...
    Each **Emotion**, ...,
        Has a "**Vibe**", we now know,
        And when measured
        By Science
            Its **Number** will show.

*Now, what **HASN'T** been told,*

    And the Reason is clear,

        Is, if your

            ***Frequency's** low*

                You cannot leave here!!

The Reasoning's plain

    As the nose on your face:

        *If your **Frequency's***

        Revved high

            You're Ascending in Space!!

*So, since **Love***

    Beats much higher

        Than hatred, or fear,

            It's the FUEL

                That powers

                    Your trip out'ta here!!!!!

There are some that will grovel
> In **Emotions** so small
>> That they hardly
>>> Will show
>>>> Any **Numbers** at all.

And, **IF** you've forgotten
> Your SOVEREIGN STATE,
>> You'll **succumb**
>>> When they dump
>>>> All their trash
>>>>> In your plate.

And they will have won
> In their quest to **CONTROL**
>> As they pull
>>> Your **Emotions**
>>>> Into a Black Hole.

But, **IF YOU REMEMBER**, ...,
    Hey! Wait! **I AM KING!**
        And I'm given
            The Power
                To Rule Everything!!!

I'll give you **NO PLACE**
    In my Frequency Band;
        For **I'm SOVEREIGN** here.
           I Rule in My Land!!

And I've **chosen** to live
    In a much higher place,
        Where there's **Love**,
           And there's **JOY**,
        And a
                More Advanced Race!

By an **ACT** of My Will
    Here I stand,
        And I've **Chosen**
            To ignore
                All those schemes
                    That your Darkness is posin'.

Take your chaos,
    Confusion,
        And all of your Fear
            That you've mongered in vain
            And just
                GET OUT OF HERE!

You have wasted your efforts,

    And taken **My** Time,

        But **The TRUTH**

            Is now plain, ...,

                That my Thoughts

                    Are DIVINE!

Yes, I've set My Intention,

    And plotted my Course,

        And I've built

            My own Rocket, ...,

                Far surpassing a Horse!

For its powered by **LOVE,**

    And I have no remorse.

        Riding Highest **"EMOTIONS",**

            I'm headed

                Toward SOURCE!!!!!!!!

Vanessa Conaway Pace
Seattle, Washington, February 5, 2005

Emotions Are Powers!!!

This Is Your Invitation To Create!

Dear Seeker of Those "Deeper Things",

The pen
    Has more might
        Than any
            Sword made;
                But We
                    Have forgotten
                        That fact,
                            I'm afraid.

So, let me
    Cajole YOU
        To take pen
            In hand,
                And write
                    What YOU"RE thinking
                    On paper,
                          (Not sand!)

And share it
    With others.
        Then THEY
            Will think, too.
                And together
                    We'll create
                        A world
                            That is new!

*Now Its YOUR Turn To Be "Creator"!
Put YOUR Thoughts Here, and Read Them Later!*

*Now Its YOUR Turn To Be "Creator"!
Put YOUR Thoughts Here, and Read Them Later!*

*Now Its YOUR Turn To Be "Creator"!
Put YOUR Thoughts Here, and Read Them Later!*

*Now Its YOUR Turn To Be "Creator"!
Put YOUR Thoughts Here, and Read Them Later!*

"Techno" Indeed!!!

www.pacepublishing.com

""Techno" Indeed!!!"
Inspirational Background

It had been a wonderful day in my Voice Studio, and now I was seeking to satisfy that craving in my sweet tooth. That new recipe for Oatmeal Cookies would do the trick. I had made it once before and they came out chewy and smelling of cinnamon, ..., my best effort so far in that field! I turned on the radio to see what the topic of discussion was for the evening. It would keep my mind occupied while my hands created some yummies.

Change seems to come when we least expect it. My world was about to be rocked, ..., yet again!

*"The only reason we need all this "technology" is that we have forgotten who we really are." What? Where did this radio guest get **that?!** Something inside me pushed my antenna up little further. I had been uncomfortable, and a little annoyed, with all of this frenzy that insisted that we must have the latest and greatest of every little gadget on the market. The advertising campaigns, the "techies" who really understood what all those changes were, and even*

the cajoling of others who succumbed to those advertising campaigns, made me feel less than "with it", and definitely second rate in the technical world, and I was, frankly, annoyed. Was it really necessary for me to buy a new TV, or a new car, every time the model changed? Was my nine-month-old computer really **that** outdated? I seemed to be getting a lot of things done on it!

The "expert in his field" went on to say that, "The only reason we need cell phones is that we have forgotten that we can communicate telepathically". Hasn't he watched **real** people lately? Maybe he doesn't have a teenager, or a Middle Management Executive in his house!

Oh, my! He was on a roll, and he kept going: "The only reason that we need airplanes is that we have forgotten that we can travel anywhere we would like to go simply by **projecting** ourselves there." Far out! The radio show guest had my undivided attention! He was describing a world that something inside me really seemed to remember. It was somehow even comfortable. Where did we lose it all? ...?

At first my mind wanted to argue with him. I was in the relative safety of my home, and he was just a nebulous voice coming out of the airwaves and into my radio. I wanted to yell out at him, "**How you do 'dat**?". But too many other things were needling my subconscious.

I had been reading some very interesting books. My friend had read them, and had said, "When you're ready, ..., I'll loan them to you". It was obvious what he meant. It was in the tone of his voice. He meant that he would release these treasures to me when I was spiritually open and mature enough to handle the messages in the book!. I knew that I was going to be in for a wild ride, ..., and I couldn't wait to get started.

He was referring to a series of books entitled "Life and Teachings of the Masters of the Far East" by Baird Spaulding. When my friend first introduced the books to me he said, "**They** are **doing** the things that we just talk about". Whoa! Talk about goading a person into a new adventure! It worked, and I am the richer for it. I borrowed Volume 1 and went directly home to get started on my new journey.

*These are not the kind of books that one just mindlessly skims through. I found myself reading a short portion, and then spending days thinking about what had just been said. Oh my! These were the well thought out reportings of Baird Spaulding, who was one of an eleven-member research team that visited the Far East for three-and-one-half years in 1894. The things they saw and experienced were far more advanced than anything **I** was doing or experiencing! The had food and provisions "miraculously" presented to them. They saw armies "miraculously" halted, and people saved from assured destruction. They heard and saw choirs of angels sing, and talked with the Wise Ones, some known to be 300 years old, and older! They experienced fellow travelers and priests bounding from the foot of awesome mountains up into the precariously placed monasteries far above them. No walking up the stairs for them! They just somehow detached themselves from the ground below and soared effortlessly up into the cliff-hanging monastery. Hmmm! And we have to build escalators and elevators! Some "advanced" society we are!*

These people didn't need elevators. And they didn't need standing armies for protection. And, they didn't need cell phones to communicate at large distances. And, they didn't even need the Cd's, i-Pods, or Internet radio to provide dinner music, or the food for the dinner, for that matter!! And when the fires and the floods came they simply fortified themselves spiritually and walked right through—unharmed. We could use some of **that** *in our everyday lives!!!*

One **should** *wonder, "Is that the only place things of that nature were happening?" And "wonder" I did! I asked questions, as I had been brought up to do. And, lo and behold, that was* **not** *the only place where they knew the ancient secrets! Books, and tapes, and Cd's, and myriads of Internet articles, and people's stories seemed to come to me from all over, each corroborating the magnificent events that the Far East researchers had written about.*

There comes a point when even the most stubbornly "educated" of us "advanced civilization" members has to throw up our "in control" hands and say, "Okay! I give! The evidence is just too overwhelming, and, besides that, my "knower" that lives inside me is giving me that "nudge" to give up managing certain parts of my universe that I have been limiting for much too long. Maybe I just need to take a quantum leap, and connect back in to the mainstream of existence."

Maybe, ..., just maybe that brave radio guest, and all those others who seemed to be confirming the Truth of his claims were trying to tell us something. Maybe, ..., just maybe, those "magic carpet rides" of our children's literature were kept around for us to see so that we would remember how we used to do it, ..., before we each had to be a two+-car family. Would we have even **bought** all those cars if we had known that we could go "over the river and through the woods to Grandmother's house" by the power of thought? What gasoline crisis??? Who would worry about the price of a barrel of oil when we could just zip on over to our destination, ..., **any** destination, ..., by just **thinking** we wanted to go there? And, why would we need all those bits-and-bytes-houses, and cell phones that mess with our bodies and the electromagnetic system of the Planet, when we already have the system within us to send all those messages **instantly** by the power of our **thoughts?**!

Wow!!! If all that is true, and it just might be, then all those science fiction writers might have been telling us something all along! Maybe they were just trying to wake up our slumbering memories! Maybe the world is full of these awesome possibilities, and all we have to do is get with the program!!!

Lemme at it!!! *In the words of the popular song, "I believe I can fly. I believe I can touch the sky"! And, ..., its quite possible, that I won't need all those technological advances to do it!*

*And what about you? Are you willing to let go of "Techno's" trappings, and soar into the **unlimited Being** that you really **ARE?!!!***

*Oh, Yes! I surely **do** have reason to feel a poem coming on!!!*

www.pacepublishing.com

Poem
"Techno" Indeed!!!

Here's a little something
    That will really make You think;
        So you'll know about the forces
            That have brought us to the brink.

Now, you thought it something wonderful
    When "**Techno**" came to town;
        And you never once considered
            It was sent to take you down!

Where you once were quite content to **pray**,
    Or **think** the problem through;
        But then, the **advertising** came,
            And said, "**We'll** do it all for you".

THEY would help you solve your problems,
    And THEY'D tell you what to think;
        If you'd only buy their product,
            It would be your missing link;

But the thought that YOU could handle
>All your needs **from deep within**
>>Is a devastating candl*
>>>That brings them a great chagrin!

If You could only see
>Just what they wanted
>>To convince,
>>>And the way
>>>>That You have **let** them,
>>>>>It would surely
>>>>>>Make you wince!

For they wanted You to think
>That You're a victim, ...,
>>What a **CRIME**
>>>To be perpetrated on
>>**A One**
>>>Descended from
>>>>**THE PRIME!!!**

You see, they tried to make You think
>That **THEY** were needed
>>All the time;
>>>And THEY tried to put a **chink**
>>>>Into the thought
>>>>>That **YOU'RE SUBLIME!!!**

But, remember where You came from.
>Keep the thought
>>That's really **True**; ...;
>>>That **The "Techno"**
>>>>That is **needed**
>>>>>Is within the heart
>>>>>>Of **YOU!!!!!!!**

For The Ancient Masters "**traveled**"
>Without bodies, ...,
>>Right through space; ...;

>>>And They're the Ones
>>>>That **we** have called
>>>>>A "**Primitivic Race**"!!!

They didn't **need** the airplanes,
    And the rockets,
        And the toys.
           They **thought**,
                And they were **there**,
                    Without a lot
                        Of useless noise!

They "**communicated**" too,
    Without the use of any wire,
        Or a tower, ...,
           Or transponder, ...,
              Without anything for **hire**!!!

And the darkness didn't stop Them;
    Nor the deadness of the night;
        For They didn't need
           An outside source, ...,
              They **were**
                  The **source** of **Light**!

And, when They wanted **Music**
    They would ask
        The Angels in to Sing,
            And They'd bask within
                That **Liquid Light**
                Of **Sound**
                      That can **form** things!

They **created** what they wanted,
    And They didn't ask a thing
        Of the ones of lesser knowing;
            For They **KNEW**
                That They were **King!!!**

Now, just what part is missing
    From Your thinking
        That **WAS** clear,
            When You roamed the stars
                By Your Own Pow'r, ...,
                    A Sovereign Chanticleer!! **

Proclaiming **Truth,** ...,
　　A **Word,** ..., A **Song,** ...,
　　　　With **manifesting pow'r**
　　　　　Of your **Intent,**
　　　　　　And by your **Voice**.....
　　　　　　　　You **knew** it every hour..

You **KNEW** that you could do it
　　With **the Pow'r that was within.**
　　　　You wouldn't even think
　　　　　　You had to bring another in.

What's happened to that **Memory**
　　Of what you used to be?
　　　　Could it be that it was hidden
　　　　With the **fact** that
　　　　　　YOU ARE FREE???

Was the plan
> To make you think
>> That you are less
>>> Than what You **ARE?**
>>> And to lie
>>>> With that old link that says
>>>>> You've fallen really far??!!

Without hope that you could ever
> Rise again, and **reconnect**
>> To **All** that Ever Was, ...,
>>> And **IS**......
>>>> **An idea**
>>>>> **That they've wrecked!**

But, the **Seed**
> That lies within You
>> Never was the dyin' kind;
>>> And now Its risen up to make
>>>> **All** that **You** have in **Mind.**

For The Mind of **One's**
> The Mind of **All,**
>> **(And Its NOT the one**
>>> **That created "The Fall"!!);**

For **IT** NEVER would make
    Anything that's less
        Than The Perfect Plan
            That's for **All** the **best,** ...,

That will take Us all through
    To loftier heights
        Where We'll learn
            To release
                All that's stored
                    In Our **Mights**.

And We won't even think
    Of the things **"Techno"** brings,
        When we **live** in our dreams,
            And our **thoughts**
                Give them wings.

When we **speak**, ...,
    And **it happens**, ...,
        We're in sync with the flow
            That wasn't quite there
                In our life
                    Down below.

There, we'd hope,
    And we'd pray,
        And there'd be a great space
            Between the time that we'd ask,
                And the time we'd embrace.

But now, We've come UP
    In the frequency band;
        Now, everything We desire
            Manifests at Command!!!

All the things that We long for
    We **attract** to ourselves;
        They exist by Our **thinking**, ...,
            Not stored on "**Techno's**" shelves!

Is it all "out there", ...,

    Waiting, ...,

        *Made by "**Techno's**" machines?*

      Or, is it ever

        ***Inside Us?* ...?**

          Life's not all as it seems!

                    Vanessa Conaway Pace
             Seattle, Washington, May 21, 2005

*(candl: a translucency indicating soundness)
**(chanter = chanter; clair = clear: One who chants clearly)

"Techno" Indeed!!!

This Is Your Invitation To Create!

Dear Seeker of Those "Deeper Things",

*In this "**Techie**" world*
    We're treadin'
        There's some things
            I'm really dreadin'
                'Bout the sleeping state
                    Our Mind's
                        Have been put in.

So, I've made some space
    To let **you**
        Write YOUR thoughts,
            And I will bet you
                Once YOU start
                    YOU'LL want
                        To do it all again!

Won't YOU join me
    With YOUR pencil, ...,
        Write "new" thoughts, ...,
            Not some old stencil, ...,
                But the feelings
                    Of YOUR Heart,
                        And Mind,
                            And Soul;

For YOU"LL find it
    Therapeutic, ...,
        Use YOUR own style
            Hermeneutic, ...,
                To interpret
                    Life around YOU
                        As a whole.

Now Its YOUR Turn To Be "Creator"!
Put YOUR Thoughts Here, and Read Them Later!

Now Its YOUR Turn To Be "Creator"!
Put YOUR Thoughts Here, and Read Them Later!

Now Its YOUR Turn To Be "Creator"!
Put YOUR Thoughts Here, and Read Them Later!

Now Its YOUR Turn To Be "Creator"!
Put YOUR Thoughts Here, and Read Them Later!

Joy Unspeakable
And Full
Of Glory

www.pacepublishing.com

"Joy Unspeakable And Full Of Glory"
Inspirational Background

"*I*'ve got joy unspeakable and full of glory," .... It was a phrase in an old chorus that we used to sing. The melody was happy, and the words uplifting, so we sang it over and over, at the top of our voices. The rafters in that old building really rang! It **felt** good! **We** felt good! It was a sure cure for the doldrums and depression! And, the best was yet to come! The "joy factor" among us rose higher and higher as that repeated happy mantra closed with the line, "and the half has never yet been told!"

Wow! If we felt that good after having heard only "half" of the message, what **would** we feel like when we heard "the rest of the story"?

I was waking up to the delightful implications of the fact that the "Real Me" is actually a three-part Being; I AM a "Spirit", and I have a Soul, and I live in a body. The "Real Me" is looking out of my eyes! Therefore, the "Real Me" is an Eternal Being that never dies! The "house" that I live in is made up of Earthly "matter", and scientific law says that "matter" changes **form**, but cannot be destroyed.

So, since We are both matter (We have a physical body) and Spirit (which is an Eternal Being), that has to mean that We have always existed!!! We were **somewhere** before We came here, and We'll be **somewhere else** if we decide not to remain here! Well now, that takes the stress out of things, doesn't it! I seems that We just can't get rid of Ourselves! Its like the T-shirt I saw that said, "Wherever I go, there I AM"!!! If we choose the pathway of death, then it's merely a transition from one state of "matter" to another, and, if we choose life in this dimension then we need to figure out what We're going to do with it! And, if we were "somewhere" before we came here, then we didn't come here as the blank slate we thought we were! (That's comforting!)

It therefore seems logical that the real "We" came here with some history, ..., some skills that we had used and developed, that suited the needs of wherever we were, and some knowledge that we garnered during those sojourns. And, it also seems logical that We had to have come here (since We are the same "life" wrapped in a different bundle of "matter") with some memories of what We felt, saw, and heard on those travels! And, it all had to have been recorded on that insatiable computer called "The Mind".

In this Technological Age that We live in maybe the computer that We ought to be studying is actually the giant computer that Dr. Valerie V. Hunt called "Infinite Mind" in her well-researched and thought-provoking study of Human Vibrations! ("Infinite Mind: Science of the Human Vibrations of Consciousness", published by Malibu Publishing Co., Malibu, California 90265.) If we could/would just connect to that **original** "Univac", then the primal memory of "the other half of the story" would rise up into our conscious level, and we would better understand the Soul's great cravings for those beauteous flowers, and colors, and Light that we came out of eons ago!

Our Souls long for Beauty in all areas of our lives. The designer longs for Beauty in the creation; the builder longs for Beauty in the execution of the design; the gardener longs for the Beauty of the garden, and the fruits of all those labors; and the singer longs for the Beauty in the music. And, the Soul of each of us longs for that Beauty of the deep friendship that holds no dangers of rejection or of being misunderstood; but, rather, embraces the wonders of the reflections of ourselves that we see in the other.

Yes! I believe we remember it all from the immense Beauty that We experienced at "Home". And, since We carry that Blueprint within Us, We are, therefore, the Ones that We have been waiting for to build a better world within and without Ourselves on this suffering Blue Planet.

So, if it's something better than this that you're looking for, just plug your "terminal" in, fire up your own "Personnel Computer", and begin downloading the stuff stored on your hard drive, ..., The **Original** One, before all those viruses of life contaminated it, and then get to work building that desired beautiful world here, based on the same universal principles that worked to create and maintain the beautiful world that you left way back "there"! We've got the technology, and We **can** do it!

We are told that computers make our work here easier and faster, ..., and, when they work, they do. But the puny computers that we struggle with here are a mere shadow of that incorruptible giant computer in the sky (or, is it really **inside of us?**). Just imagine what We could accomplish if We actually achieved a clear connection to **that** one!!!

"All downloads are complete!"

Now, all we have to do is live it out!

*Oh! **That's** where the dangers lie. It would all be automatic if it weren't for that little thing called "free will". Now **I have to decide** whether I will follow the original Manufacturer's instructions for my "computer", or whether I'll say, in the words of the old song, "I did it **my** way". We'll know what We decided to do by the quantity and quality of the Beauty that We created!*

Oops! There's that connection! ...! I feel a poem coming on, ...,

www.pacepublishing.com

Poem
Joy Unspeakable and Full of Glory!!

Surround yourself
        With **Beauty;**

Surround yourself
        With **Love;**

        And you'll build
            A little picture here
                Of how it is "***above***"!

Where there's **Love**

        And **Laughter** shining

        In the Gleam of every eye,
            And there's **Information** flowing
                With no need to question "Why?"

Yes, there's **Order**;

    And there's **Singing,** ...,

        "Sounds" exalted and profound,

            That we're longing soooo

                To hear once more, ...,

                    They're missing

                        On this ground!!

In the meantime

    We can **Build** it

        In this world to which we've come

            With the **Flowers,**

                Light, and **Colors**

                Of the **Glories** left

                    At "Home";

And with **Friends** like you
    Who share, and dream,
        And grow by leaps and bounds,
            And transform every "negative"
              To **Musical Love Sounds!!!**

We can fashion every moment
    To be just the way we want
        To be filled with **Life**,
           And **Love**,
              And **Peace**
                In our world
                  Called **"Jubilant"!!**

So, Surround yourself
   *With **Beauty**;*
And Surround yourself
   *With **Love**;*
      *And **build** a little picture here*
         *Of how it is **"above"**!*

Vanessa Conaway Pace
Seattle, Washington, December 11, 2004

Joy Unspeakable and Full of Glory!!

This Is Your
Invitation
To Create!

Dear Seeker of Those "Deeper Things",

There's something in
    The Hu-man soul
        That wants to be
           A poet;

So, all you do
    Is go "inside",
        Then write it down,
           And show it!!!

Now Its YOUR Turn To Be "Creator"!
Put YOUR Thoughts Here, and Read Them Later!

Now Its YOUR Turn To Be "Creator"!
Put YOUR Thoughts Here, and Read Them Later!

Now Its YOUR Turn To Be "Creator"!
Put YOUR Thoughts Here, and Read Them Later!

Now Its YOUR Turn To Be "Creator"!
Put YOUR Thoughts Here, and Read Them Later!

Whatever Happened To "Me"?

The International Library of Poetry,
Editor's Choice Award, 2005

www.pacepublishing.com

"Whatever Happened To "Me"?"
Inspirational Background

My Voice Student had worked hard at the Nursing Home that day. She always came in tired for her lesson. Actual hands-on nursing is always fatiguing, but it is especially so in a Nursing Home. Situations are usually dire, and the resources, both within the patient, and within the system, are often stretched beyond any reasonable hope.

Today had been one of "those days" for this Voice Student. Singing takes a lot of energy and concentration, and my experience as a Voice Teacher has taught me that the Soul must be freed before the Voice can soar, so, before we could sing, the story would need to be brought out. I listened.

An elderly lady had come into the Nursing Home to recuperate from a hip replacement surgery. Something wasn't working right, so she was taken back to the hospital to fix the problem. She was then returned to the Nursing Home for the care and attention that she needed during recovery. But, again, something had gone terribly wrong. When she was being turned in her bed it seemed that somehow someone picked her weight up by her leg, and that strain on the hip joint pulled the newly replaced hip joint out of its socket (my understanding of the situation as she described it). Life had definitely taken a turn for the worse. There would be more trips to the hospital, and the prognosis did not look good.

The future was looking pretty bleak---unless a miracle happened. Her problem came suddenly. She had, of course, never planned that life would take such a turn. But it started me thinking about the importance of taking the bull by the horns WHILE WE HAVE TODAY, and turning our "dreams" of what we would like to do into a list of things that we have already done.

One of my favorite sayings comes from Admiral David Glasgow Farragut (1801-1870) who refused to look at the obstacles in front of his ship because he had a mission to fulfill. **So do each of us!!** His courageous, "Damn the torpedoes. Full speed ahead." has egged me on many times when "obstacles" would have held back my forward progress.

The saying actually means to "advance without hesitation". So, when things get in the way of accomplishing your hopes and dreams just pass by those opportunities to be stopped. The TRUTH is that **We create what we want. So, go to it!!! Create what you want!!! No better day than today to dust off those old dreams and decide that you are going to accomplish them. Having made the decision, just watch the supply come seeking for you, as you take the necessary steps toward knowing the joy of accomplishing your dreams!!!**

CREATE SOMETHING BEAUTIFUL YOURSELF EVERY DAY!

My Student was grieved on a Hu-man level at the great suffering that the woman was experiencing.

Eventually we were able to work through her almost debilitating grief for the woman to the point that she was able to begin to sing. Music, and singing in particular, is a marvelous healing tool, and by the time she left the Music had done its magic, and she was exhilarated, and better able to deal with the realities of this patient's injuries on both a practical physical level, and as a compassionate comforter. Of course, her training stood her in good stead on a professional level, and she knew exactly what to do for the precious lady on that level, but something within us so relates to the emotional pain of others around us that we often have to pull ourselves up out of the doldrums before we can be of any help to the actual sufferer. Medicine can treat the wound, and prescribe a pill, but how do you heal a broken heart, or give hope when there doesn't seem to be any? We're really on the outside looking in.

The lesson was over, and my Student had gone home. I was alone in the Studio, and trying to finish the day's work, ..., but the story wouldn't leave my mind. I began to **feel** the hopelessness and the grief that precious woman was feeling. I could **feel** her grappling with the idea that life, at least as she had known it, was slipping by, and I could **feel** the heavy mourning of dreams unfulfilled.

I feel the wail of a poem coming on..... No!...! It's the Song of a grieving Soul singing out the remorse of a life unfulfilled. There is no greater sorrow.

Poem
Whatever Happened To "Me"?

Whatever happened
    To the **Plans** I had
      For "M**e**"?

Whatever happened
    To the **Gift** that I
      Would **be**?

Whatever happened
    To the **Life** that I
      Would **see**?

    Oh,
        Whatever happened
      To "**Me**"?

Whatever happened
 *To all the **Dreams***
  I planned?

Whatever happened
 *To the **Gifts** I had*
  In hand?

Whatever happened
 *To the **Plans** that were*
  So grand?

Oh,
 Whatever happened
  *To "**Me**"?*

Once I had hopes
    And a future,
        And plans
            For just what I would **be;**

But now,
    All the facts
        Point to "loser",
            While **Talents,**
                And **Gifts,**
                    And **Plans**
                        Sleep in **"Me"**!!!

Oh, how did I miss
    What I'd planned for?
        And why did I not
            Pay the price,
                To **be** all those things
                    I should stand for,

              And to **live**
                  In **Divine Paradise?**

Oh,
    Whatever happened
        To "Me"?

      Oh,
          Whatever happened
            To "Me"?

Vanessa Conaway Pace
Seattle, Washington, 1998

Song

Whatever Happened To "Me"?

Vanessa Conaway Pace
Vanessa Conaway Pace

1997

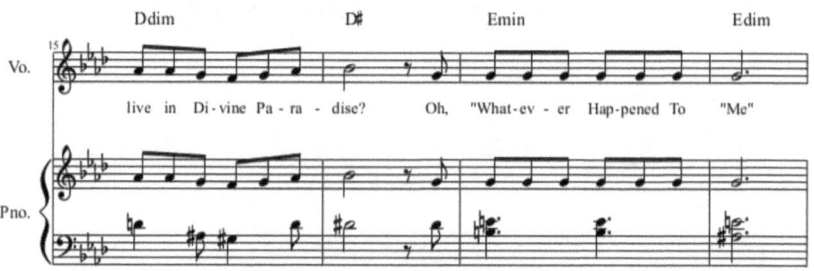

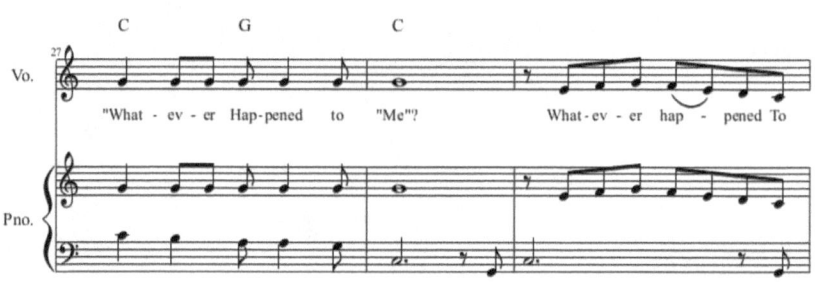

www.pacepublishing.com

Whatever Happened To "Me"?

This Is *Your* Invitation To Create!

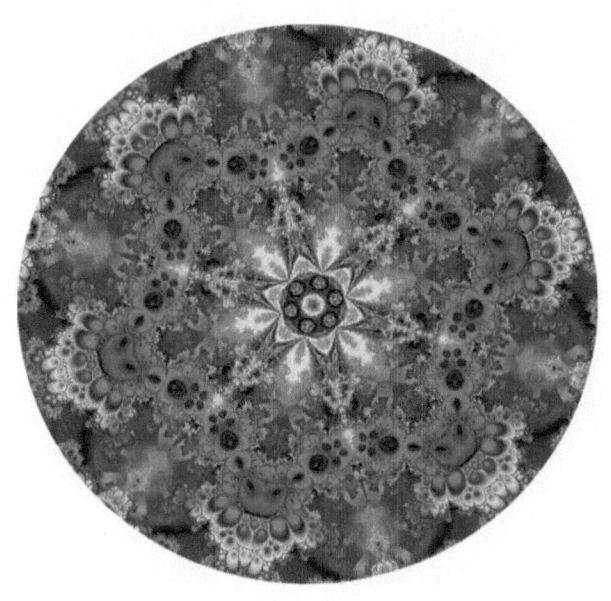

Dear Seeker of Those "Deeper Things",

There are "Moments"
    In life,
        And **that's**
            Where We **live**.

In the depths
    Of Our feelings
        We'll find something
            To give.

So, reach down
    And share
        Thoughts with meaning
            To YOU,

And YOU"ll find
    That those same thoughts
        Will touch
            Others, too!

Now Its YOUR Turn To Be "Creator"!
Put YOUR Thoughts Here, and Read Them Later!

Now Its YOUR Turn To Be "Creator"!
Put YOUR Thoughts Here, and Read Them Later!

Now Its YOUR Turn To Be "Creator"!
Put YOUR Thoughts Here, and Read Them Later!

Now Its YOUR Turn To Be "Creator"!
Put YOUR Thoughts Here, and Read Them Later!

Somewhere There's An Answer

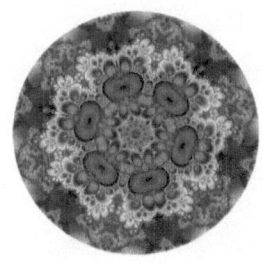

www.pacepublishing.com

"Somewhere There's An Answer"
Inspirational Background

Have you ever been presented with an idea or statement that your spirit knew was not True? I guess We all have, so the question becomes, **how do we handle it?** How do we get the strength to follow that Still Small Voice from within when we are being bombarded with statements that are being made by people, and teachings that we may have accepted as an authoritative source in our lives?

When I was first told that I am King over my life, I immediately thought about the Kings that we have read about in history, and how they **ruled** over their subjects. Now, I am being told that I am King over my own life. Even the most benevolent King is, by definition, still **ruler over others**. In my mind **Love** would never do that. The idea of one Hu-man Being ruling over another Hu-man Being is totally contrary to the whole concept of **Love**. Indeed, it is an odious idea! **Love** serves its object with the greatest respect for for its value and sovereignty; it does **not rule** over it. And, if we are, indeed, All One, then who has the right to appoint another, or to deem himself superior to, and therefore ruler over, another "Part" of **The One**? No, there was **definitely** something wrong with the teaching surrounding this Kingship idea.

But, the answer is kind of hard to handle.

We had also been told that we sort of came here by default, ..., a victim of the Great Lottery in Sky, ..., that we had no say in the matter, and that we'd just have to accept the luck of the draw. That teaching spawned a "victim" mentality, and that festered into a full-blown, although sometimes deeply buried and well-hidden, resentment at our seemingly unchangeable fate.

In my mind I **KNEW** that **Love** wouldn't do **that** either. So, I needed an answer.

Justice may be turned away backward in the current conditions in which we live, but it could not have been that way in the **real** beginning, in which we all shared. I know that True Love respects the Sovereignty of others; therefore, we could not have been sent here without our permission! And, in order for us to give our permission we would have **had** to have had full knowledge of what was happening to us, and been fully involved in the Planning of this excursion. And, **Love** would **not** do anything without a perfect reason; so, that would mean that there was a definite reason for making all the effort that it took to get us here. .... You think it didn't take effort?! We spend days, weeks, and even years planning and preparing for a vacation trip here; just imagine the meticulous planning and preparation that we would have to make for our trip to Planet Earth!!!

All **that** would indicate that we had to have had some responsibility for the terms and conditions of our arrival in the flesh here on our spaceship called Earth. It would also mean that We had, and have, the ability, and the responsibility, to successfully accomplish every part of The Plan that we purposefully came here to do! We must be willing to manage ourselves, and to bring all those warring factions within Ourselves into agreement, so that we can **live** in Our own Peaceable Kingdom.

That's what True Kings do! They **manage** the Kingdom **inside** of them! They rule and reign over the many "person-alities" (such as, old ideas, emotional responses, and physical conditions) that are vying for the throne of their lives! A "Kingdom divided" cannot stand, so, as True Kings, **not over others**, but over the Kingdom **within Us**, We must soothe the savage beasts **within Us** that seek to destroy us, and we must nourish the True Royalty that We really **ARE!**

Wow! I **AM** a King! And I'm **not** looking for a Kingdom. I already **AM** one! ...! My triumphant Soul **SHALL** Sing!

I **definitely** feel a poem coming on!

Poem
Somewhere There's An Answer

Where is the answer
    To all of Life's Plan?
        Is there more
            To our coming
                Than just
                      Being "Man"?

Are there worlds
    We can conquer,
        And dreams
            We can share?
                Was there Joy
                    When we wrote
                      All the Plans
                          We made "there"?

Was there singing,
    And laughter,
        As we made
            The Great Plan?
                Or, were we just
                    Downright **curious**
                        As to the work
                            Of our hand?

Somewhere there's an Answer
    We're all looking to find;
        And **together**
            We'll have it,
                For we're all
                      The same kind!

The riches we cherished,

    And the **Joy**

        That we've known

           Are all part

              Of our **Being**

                  That **we brought here**

                    From "Home".

So spread

    The good news

        Of the riches We bring,

           For We're **given this Life**

                Over which

                    YOU are King!!!

Vanessa Conaway Pace
Seattle, Washington, July 2004

www.pacepublishing.com

Somewhere There's An Answer

***This Is** Your*
Invitation
To Create!

Dear Seeker of Those "Deeper Things",

Dare to ask questions,
    And then,
        Write them down.
            YOU might find
                That the answers
                    Will bring YOU
                        A frown!

But, sharing
    The process
        Of thinking
            It through,
                Will help
                    Inspire others
                        To think things
                            Through, too!

Now Its YOUR Turn To Be "Creator"!
Put YOUR Thoughts Here, and Read Them Later!

Now Its YOUR Turn To Be "Creator"!
Put YOUR Thoughts Here, and Read Them Later!

Now Its YOUR Turn To Be "Creator"!
Put YOUR Thoughts Here, and Read Them Later!

Now Its YOUR Turn To Be "Creator"!
Put YOUR Thoughts Here, and Read Them Later!

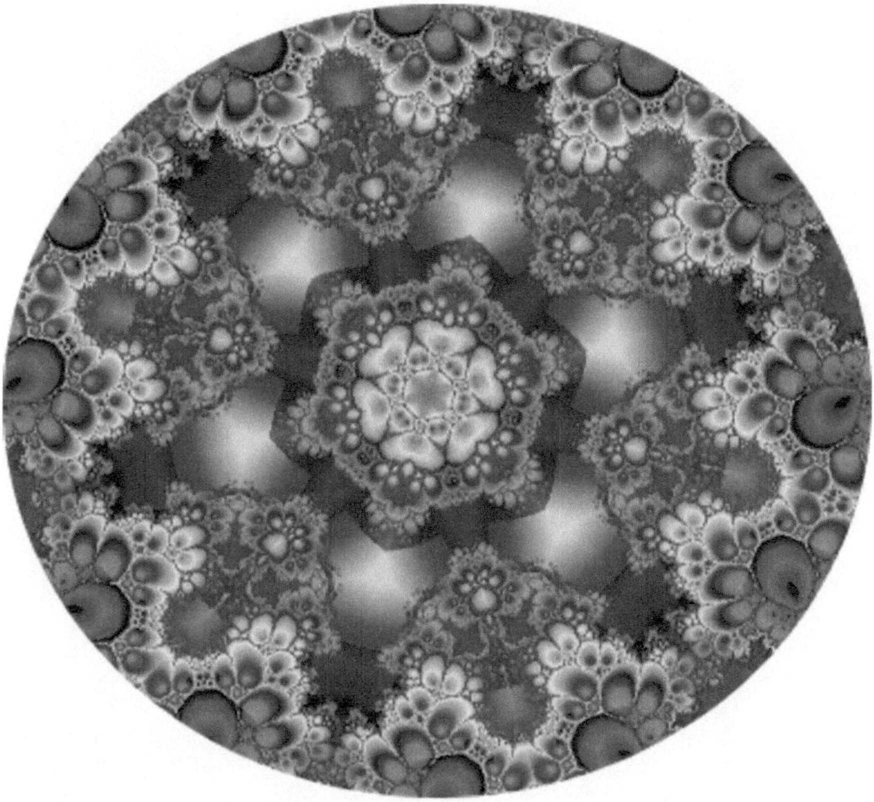

Preparing
The REAL ME!!

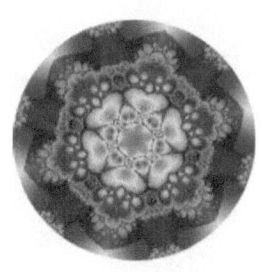

www.pacepublishing.com

"Preparing The REAL ME!!"
Inspirational Background

"*The Subconscious Song*" (about which we read previously in this book) had been stirring in me for several days, but, somehow we Hu-mans don't catch on very fast. We are so busy, doing what we think is important, that We sometimes miss the subtle gems that the Still Small Voice within Us is trying to give Us.

There it was again, ..., that haunting tune, singing itself inside Me, with words that were awakening Me to yet another eternal Truth!

I had been seeking answers to critically important questions in my life. I knew that "**Love**" would not just throw us down here and tell us to "Do the best you can with what you've got"! "**Somewhere There's An Answer**" (as we read in the previous poem). I just had to find it, ..., rather, **them**!

Does it really matter what I **do** here? Is it really important for Me to think **only** on the things I would really like to have happen? Are my words **really** that important? So what if I blow up in a fit of anger once in a while? Will the sky fall in? What if I just want to sit here and cry because I have been hurt so deeply? Why can't I strike back when the bullies maul me over? Why do **I** have to walk in integrity when so much of the world does not, ..., and seems to get away with it? Why do I have to forgive others, when it's perfectly clear that **they** have done me wrong? Why do I have to **Love** those whom I feel have walked through my life with spiked boots?

There it was again, ..., another **book**! (I am so grateful to my "friends" who are the many authors who have paid the price to faithfully share their hard-earned studies and revelations in the books and articles that have helped me grow.) I don't even know how that book got to me, but all of a sudden I was aware of its being in my library. It was one of those little books that you can read in an hour, and then spend the rest of your life living it out. It was called "The Pharisee In Me", and it talked about the higher life that we can attain. For some, who just want to "get by" in this life, they could slough off on things of integrity, ... but, for those of us who held a higher ideal, that wasn't an option.

Why is it that some of us get caught doing the simplest little thing that is "wrong", when others seem to get away with doing massively "wrong" things? The seasoned author of "The Pharisee In Me" had been well tempered to a higher walk in life, and the answer to my flippant question shouted off the page to me: **"It's okay for them, but for you it's not okay, because you have set a higher standard for yourself"**. Oh. I get it.

Didn't like the message much. It meant that I was going to have to knuckle down, and manage Me, my emotions, my thoughts, and my doings, and bring them all in line with the higher Laws of the universe. Then, I will **become** what I am willing to govern according to the guidelines of a Virtuous Hu-man Being. And, I am coming to know that once I make the decision to walk in that, all the Help I need will be at my beckon call! We're NOT alone! Not now, ..., not ever!!!

Wow! There **is** hope for Me yet!

Now I do hear a poem coming on, ..., and one with a message so important as this must have **The Power of Music** with it! Won't you sing it with me?

www.pacepublishing.com

Poem
Preparing the REAL ME!!

I AM becoming
> What *I* will be
>> In Eternity.

Every decision
> That *I* make here
>> Forms *I*-dentity!

When this Life is over
> *I* will ever be
>> What *I* have decided **here**
>>> To change in me!

CHORUS:
While *I AM*
> Upon the Earth
>> *I'll* do my part

To prepare
> The **REAL ME**
>> Within my heart

That will live forever
> That will always be
>> The "**ME**" that *I* designed to be
>>> Right from the start!

I decide
    *What **I** will be*
        Forevermore.
Each reaction, ...,
    Every thought, ...,
        ***I** place in store*
    Every act performed now
        Will turn out to be
            A brick
                That builds My Mansion
                For Eternity!

CHORUS:

*While **I AM***
    Upon the Earth
        ***I'll** do my part*
To prepare
    *The **REAL ME***
        Within my heart
That will live forever
    That will always be
        *The "**ME**" that **I** designed to be*
        Right from the start!

Every thought
    Allowed to linger
        In My heart
            Adds another Level to
                My wondrous start, …,
                    Fixing and transforming
                        The **Life I** want to be,
                            The Being that
                                I'll shine as
                                    Through Eternity!!

CHORUS:

While **I AM**
    Upon the Earth
        I'll do my part
To prepare
    The **REAL ME**
        Within my heart
    That will live forever
    That will always be
        The "**ME**" that **I** designed to be
            Right from the start!

The friend We choose now
    Is the friend
        We know We need,
    Who holds the keys
        To bring Us
            Up to par with speed!
    We'll see Our **reflection**
        In others that We see
            Because We're all a part
                Of **One Big Family!!**

CHORUS:

While **I AM**
    Upon the Earth
        I'll do my part
    To prepare
        The **REAL ME**
            Within my heart
        That will live forever
        That will always be
            The "**ME**" that **I** designed to be
            Right from the start!

Vanessa Conaway Pace
Seattle, Washington, July 2004

Song

Preparing The REAL ME!!

Vanessa Conaway Pace Vanessa Conaway Pace

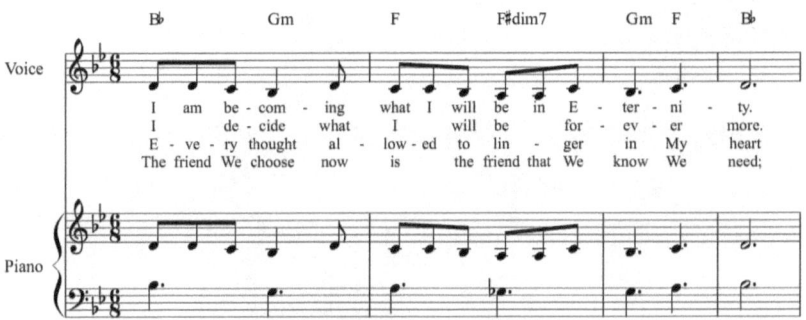

I am be-com-ing what I will be in E-ter-ni-ty.
I de-cide what I will be for-ev-er more.
E-ve-ry thought al-low-ed to lin-ger in My heart
The friend We choose now is the friend that We know We need;

Ev-'ry de-ci-sion that I make here forms I-den-ti-
Each re-ac-tion,..., E-ve-ry thought,... I place in
Adds an-oth-er le-vel to My won-drous
Who holds the keys to bring Us up to par with

2013

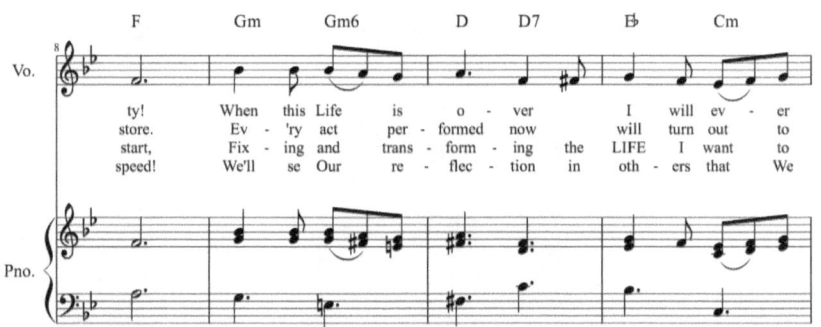

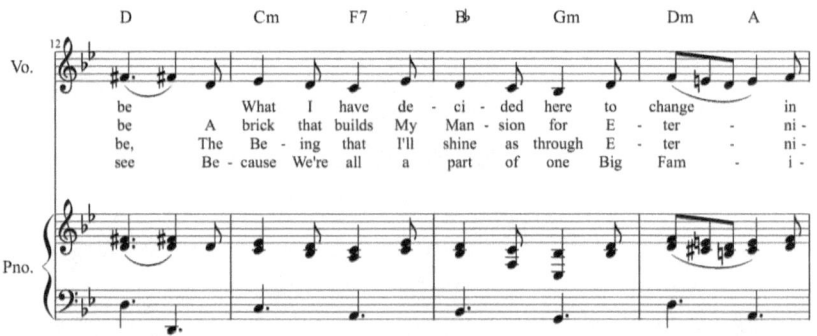

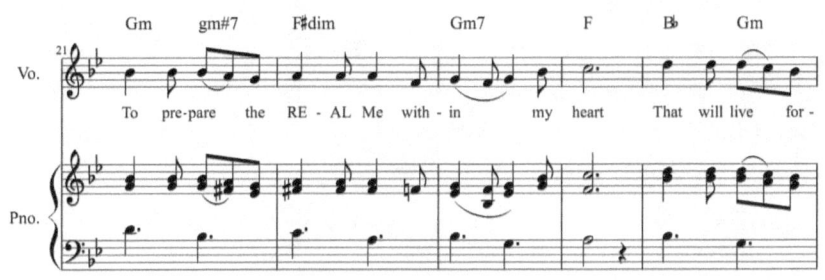

Preparing the REAL ME!!

This Is your Invitation To Create!

Dear Seeker of Those "Deeper Things",

So, make
      Your own music,
           And sing
                  Your own song,
                      And help share
                            The Beauty
                                For which
                                    We all long.

It comes
      From the thoughts
           On the inside
                Of YOU,
                      So, We need
                          Everyone,
                              To DO
                                  What YOU
                                      Can DO!

Now Its YOUR Turn To Be "Creator"!
Put YOUR Thoughts Here, and Read Them Later!

*Now Its YOUR Turn To Be "Creator"!
Put YOUR Thoughts Here, and Read Them Later!*

Now Its YOUR Turn To Be "Creator"!
Put YOUR Thoughts Here, and Read Them Later!

Now Its YOUR Turn To Be "Creator"!
Put YOUR Thoughts Here, and Read Them Later!

Epilogue

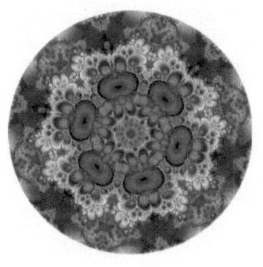

www.pacepublishing.com

Epilogue

Now that We
 Have shared this cup,
  There is more to come,
   So, listen up!
    Another book
     Is coming soon,
      So I hope you
       Will stay
        In tune,

So that We
 Can share again
  Some thoughts
   That help Us all begin
    Another climb
     On another day
      To head Us on
       The upward way,

Where We
 Will meet,
  As Our Minds join,
   As We seek
    To live
     By Spirit's "coin",

And We think
 On things
  Of some import,
   So that,
    In the end,
     We won't
      Come up short

On the cosmic scale
    By which we're judged,
        And we won't
            Have to lean
                On some facts
                    That are "fudged",

But, rather,
    We'll **all** land
        On Our feet
           In that Love filled
              "*Home*"
                  Where Life's
                      Really neat!!!

See You
    In Volume Two!!!

                      Vanessa Conaway Pace
            Lynnwood, Washington, September 21, 2013

Epilogue

This Is Your *Invitation To Create!*

Dear Seeker of Those "Deeper Things",

So, write
      YOUR dreams here,
          And Sing
              Everywhere,
                  And make up a Poem, ...,
                  YOU have
                      Something
                          To share,

To bring out
      The Beauty
           That's inside
                Of YOU!

                We're all here,
                    And We're waiting, ...,
                        And We're counting
                            On YOU!!!

Now Its YOUR Turn To Be "Creator"!
Put YOUR Thoughts Here, and Read Them Later!

Now Its YOUR Turn To Be "Creator"!
Put YOUR Thoughts Here, and Read Them Later!

Now Its YOUR Turn To Be "Creator"!
Put YOUR Thoughts Here, and Read Them Later!

Now Its YOUR Turn To Be "Creator"!
Put YOUR Thoughts Here, and Read Them Later!

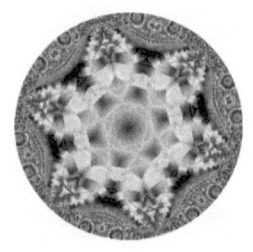

Reading List

www.pacepublishing.com

Interesting Books To Reflect Upon

TITLE	AUTHOR	PUBLISHER	LOCATION
Awakening to Zero Point: The Collective Initiation	Gregg Braden	Radio Bookstore Press	Bellevue, WA
Cosmic Music: Musical Keys to the Interpretation of Reality	Joscelyn Godwin	Inner Traditions International	Rochester, VT
Cymatics: A Study of Wave Phenomena	Hans Jenny	Macromedia	
Go Within Or Go Without	Gloria D. Benich	Miracle Publishing Co.	Stevensville, MI
Healing and Regeneration Through Music	Corinne Heline	DeVorss & Company	Marina del Rey, CA
Healing Codes for the Biological Apocalypse	Leonard G. Horowitz	Healthy World Distributors	Las Vegas, NV
Health and Light	Dr. John N. Ott	Simon & Schuster, Inc.	New York, NY
Infinite Mind: Science of the Human Vibrations of	Dr. Valerie V. Hunt	Malibu Publishing Co.	Malibu, CA

Consciousness		
Life and Teaching of the Masters of the Far East (Volumes 1-6)	Baird T. Spalding	DeVorss Publications	Marina del Rey, CA
Love Thyself: The Message from Water III	Dr. Masuro Emoto	Hay House, Inc.	Carlsbad, CA
Messages From Water (Volume 1)	Dr. Masuro Emoto	Hado Publishing,	Tokyo, Japan
Messages from Water (Volume 2)	Dr. Masuro Emoto	Sunmark Pub	Tokyo, Japan
Music, Mysticism and Magic: A Sourcebook	Joscelyn Godwin	ARKANA/Viking Penguin, Inc.	New York, NY
Peace-Power and Plenty	Orison Swett Marden	Thomas Y. Crowell Company	New York, New York
Power vs. Force	Dr. David Hawkins	Veritas	Sedona, AZ
Quantum Healing: Exploring the Frontiers of Mind/Body Medicine	Deepak Chopra, M.D.	Bantam Books	New York, NY
Sacred Sounds	Ted Andrews	Llewellyn Publications	Woodbury, MN

The Angels Within Us	John Randolph Price	Fawcett Columbine	New York, New York
The Body Electric	Robert O. Becker,	William Morrow	New York, NY
The Genius Frequency: An Owner's Manual for the Cosmic Mind	John J. Falone	Global Light Network	Virginia Beach, VA
The Hidden Messages in Water	Dr. Masuro Emoto	Atria Books	New York, NY
The Man Who Tapped The Secrets Of The Universe	Glenn Clark	The University of Science and Philosophy (The Walter Russell Foundation)	Waynesboro, VA
The Mozart Effect	Don Campbell	Avon Books	New York, NY
The Mozart Effect for Children	Don Campbell	Harper Collins	New York, NY
The Mysticism of Sound and Music: The Sufi Teaching of	Hazrat Inayat Khan	Shambhala Dragon Editions	Boston and London
The Secret Life of Water	Dr. Masuro Emoto	Atria Books	New York, NY

The Secret Lore of Music	Fabre d'Olivet	Inner Traditions International	Rochester, VT
The Secret of Light	Walter Russell	University of Science and Philosophy (The Walter Russell Foundation)	Waynesboro, VA
The Secret Power of Music	David Tame	Destiny Books	Rochester, VT
The Secret Teachings of all Ages	Manly P. Hall	Dover Publications	Mineola, NY
The Superbeings	John Randolph Price	Fawcett Columbine	New York, New York
The True Power of Water	Dr. Masuro Emoto	Beyond Words Publishing	Hillsboro, OR
Vibrational Medicine	Dr. Richard Gerber	Inner Traditions/Bear & Company	Rochester, VT
When God Was a Woman	Merlin Stone	Dorset Press	New York, NY

www.thewondersofmusic.com

Request for Reader's Review

There's a "Poet"
    That's living
        On the inside
            Of YOU!!!

And Its speaking
    For The One
        That lives in Me
            TOO!

Hoping You
    Have enjoyed
        All these Books
            Through and through,

And that You'd
    Be so kind
        As to write
            A Review!!!

And to post it
    To Amazon's

       Page for this Book
          So that others
              Will know
                    To give THIS BOOK
                        A LOOK!!!

And maybe
    You'll send it
        To this "Poet"
           TOO!

So I can say
    "Thank You"
        For seeing that
           Through!!!

            This Poet,
       and The Poetry Muses,
     and all the new Readers
who are searching for this material
        will Thank You!!!

For
    Concerts that make
        You Laugh and Cry,

    Creative products
        That You'll want to buy,

    Poetry that makes
        You see new things,

    And Wisdom on Voice
        That'll help You Sing!

Contact Vanessa Pace at
    www.pacepublishing.com
        Post Office Box 2187, Lynnwood, WA 98036

www.pacepublishing.com

www.ingramcontent.com/pod-product-compliance
Lightning Source LLC
Chambersburg PA
CBHW030439300426
44112CB00009B/1068